Rev. Rhodes writes with a humble, clear, concise grasp of Scripture and the Reformed faith. I found myself deeply appreciative of the theological depth and scriptural richness that he brings to this discussion of worship. At various times I was encouraged, convicted, instructed, and refreshed in ways that have increased—and I hope will continue to increase—my faith in and my appreciation of a God who meets us so powerfully and so practically in such ordinary and available means of grace. This book reminds us how amazing it is that such grace is available to us each and every time we assemble ourselves together for corporate worship.

—**Duane Cory**, Founding Pastor, Deer Creek Church, Littleton, Colorado

Our hearts are often cold and closed to the supernatural wonder of corporate worship. But thanks to Jonty Rhodes's warm style and compelling argumentation, *Reformed Worship* will melt your heart and draw you to the duty and delight that is meeting with God. This book will make you long for Sunday, even heaven.

—**Jonathan Landry Cruse**, Pastor, Community Presbyterian Church, Kalamazoo, Michigan

Jonty reminds us of the biblical and systematic theology that undergirds a Reformed view of worship. But he also writes for the punter in the pew, not just the pastor in the pulpit. The book is clear, accessible, winsome, and practical. The last chapter especially will be of immense help to those who have remaining questions about the practical side of Reformed worship. This is a book I'll be recommending to many people for many years to come.

—**Jonny Gibson**, Associate Professor of Old Testament, Westminster Theological Seminary; coeditor, *Reformation Worship*

A biblical, coherent, and engaging summary of Reformed worship. Rhodes has provided the church with a wonderful foundation for understanding how God calls his people to worship according to his redemptive work and his revealed Word.

—**Brian Salter**, Lead Pastor, Lookout Mountain Presbyterian Church, Lookout Mountain, Tennessee

In this wonderful little book, Jonty Rhodes commends the unique characteristics of Reformed worship. Rather than playing the critic of sloppy or unbiblical worship, Rhodes accessibly and positively presents a Reformed approach to our highest calling. Reformed conviction focuses on how Christ mediates our worship and graciously provides in his Word the means by which God's people are to worship him. In his clear and witty style, Rhodes not only informs in this book—he also inspires the reader to pursue the blessings of Reformed worship.

—**D. Blair Smith**, Associate Professor of Systematic Theology, Reformed Theological Seminary, Charlotte; Academic Dean, Reformed Theological Seminary, Dallas and Houston

REFORMED
WORSHIP

BLESSINGS OF THE FAITH
A Series

Jason Helopoulos
Series Editor

Covenantal Baptism, by Jason Helopoulos
Expository Preaching, by David Strain
Persistent Prayer, by Guy M. Richard
Reformed Theology, by Jonathan Master
Reformed Worship, by Jonty Rhodes

"Jason Helopoulos has assembled a fine team
of God-centered authors who are anchored
in his Word and lovers of his church."
Sinclair B. Ferguson

REFORMED

WORSHIP

JONTY RHODES

P U B L I S H I N G
P.O. BOX 817 • PHILLIPSBURG • NEW JERSEY 08865-0817

Printed in the United States of America

Library of Congress Cataloging-in-Publication Data

Names: Rhodes, Jonty (Clergy), author.
Title: Reformed worship / Jonty Rhodes.
Description: Phillipsburg, New Jersey : P&R Publishing, [2023] | Series:
  Blessings of the faith | Includes bibliographical references. | Summary:
  "Writing with winsome enthusiasm, Jonty Rhodes celebrates the simplicity
  and freedom of Reformed worship. Discover the excitement of meeting with
  God in the means and manner he promises to bless"-- Provided by
  publisher.
Identifiers: LCCN 2023000775 | ISBN 9781629959078 (hardcover) | ISBN
  9781629959108 (epub)
Subjects: LCSH: Public worship--Reformed Church. | Worship--Biblical
  teaching.
Classification: LCC BX9427 .R49 2023 | DDC 264/.042--dc23/eng/20230315
LC record available at https://lccn.loc.gov/2023000775

For little Iona

May you join your family around the throne in worship

And with grateful thanks to Matthew, David, Paul, and Jonny, from whom I've learned so much and to whom I can always turn

CONTENTS

FOREWORD

It has often been said—sometimes with a sense of humor and sometimes in annoyance—that Presbyterian and Reformed churches love to do things "decently and in order." I can understand both the humor and the frustration that lie behind that sentiment. We love our plans, our minutes, our courts, and our committees. Presbyterian and Reformed folks have been known to appoint committees just to oversee other committees (reminding me of the old *Onion* headline that announced "New Starbucks Opens in Rest Room of Existing Starbucks"). We like doing things so decently that we expect our church officers to know three things: the Bible, our confessions, and a book with *Order* in its title.

But before we shake our heads in disbelief at those uber-Reformed types (physician, heal thyself!), we should recall that before "decently and in order" was a Presbyterian predilection, it was a biblical command (see 1 Cor. 14:40). Paul's injunction for the church to be marked by propriety and decorum, to be well-ordered like troops drawn up in ranks, is a fitting conclusion to a portion of Scripture that deals with confusion regarding gender, confusion at the Lord's Table, confusion about spiritual gifts, confusion in the body of Christ, and confusion in public worship. "Decently and in order" sounds pretty good compared to the mess that prevailed in Corinth.

A typical knock on Presbyterian and Reformed Christians is that though supreme in head, they are deficient in heart. We are the emotionless stoics, the changeless wonders, God's frozen chosen. But such veiled insults would not have impressed the apostle Paul, for he knew that the opposite of order in the church is not free-flowing spontaneity; it is self-exalting chaos. God never favors confusion over peace (see 1 Cor. 14:33). He never pits theology against doxology or head against heart. David Garland put it memorably: "The Spirit of ardor is also the Spirit of order."[1]

When Jason Helopoulos approached me about writing a foreword for this series, I was happy to oblige—not only because Jason is one of my best friends (and we both root for the hapless Chicago Bears) but because these careful, balanced, and well-reasoned volumes will occupy an important place on the book stalls of Presbyterian and Reformed churches. We need short, accessible books written by thoughtful, seasoned pastors for regular members on the foundational elements of church life and ministry. That's what we need, and that's what this series delivers:

wise answers to many of the church's most practical and pressing questions.

This series of books on Presbyterian and Reformed theology, worship, and polity is not a multivolume exploration of 1 Corinthians 14:40, but I am glad it is unapologetically written with Paul's command in mind. The reality is that every church will worship in some way, pray in some way, be led in some way, be structured in some way, and do baptism and the Lord's Supper in some way. Every church is living out some form of theology—even if that theology is based on pragmatism instead of biblical principles. Why wouldn't we want the life we share in the church to be shaped by the best exegetical, theological, and historical reflections? Why wouldn't we want to be thoughtful instead of thoughtless? Why wouldn't we want all things in the life we live together to be done decently and in good order? That's not the Presbyterian and Reformed way. That's God's way, and Presbyterian and Reformed Christians would do well not to forget it.

Kevin DeYoung
Senior Pastor, Christ Covenant Church
Matthews, North Carolina

Introduction

WELCOME IN

Invited up front by the friendly, well-meaning pastor, I looked out over a church perhaps ten times the size of my own. The elders joined us on the platform, and I was ushered front and center. At a nod from the music director, the congregation, pastor, and elders began to sing. No hymnbooks. No service sheets. No words projected on a screen. Everyone knew what to do. Well, nearly everyone. To this day I have no idea what they were singing. I *think* it was in Latin. I stood on the platform, moved my lips, guppy-fish style, and pretended I knew what was going on.

Perhaps you've had a similar experience. Worship styles, indeed worship services, vary hugely from church to church, even among Bible-trusting, evangelical Christians. They can at times leave us baffled. There are organs and electric guitars, choirs and praise bands, pastors in hipster jeans, pastors in suits, and pastors in robes straight out of the seventeenth century. There are formal services with heavily structured liturgies and video-montage peppered "events" with donut breaks and puppet shows. What are we to make of all this? Is it the inevitable and welcome outcome of cultural diversity? A case of Pick 'n' Mix Christianity, where everyone chooses their favorite flavor, no rights, no wrongs? Or might there be something more substantial at stake?

I hope this short book will persuade you of the latter—that worship matters. Not just *that* we worship; almost every Christian would agree on that. But that *how* we worship matters.

Straightaway I realize that might make some readers nervous. Haven't we had enough of the "worship wars," the interminable bickering between Christians who profess to love one another? Do we really need another pastor to wade into the action to strike left, right, and center at anyone who does things slightly differently from him? If you're among those nervous readers, then let me reassure you: the pages that follow won't be a demolition job of other tribes and traditions. Instead I'd like to show you around the house I live in: the house of Reformed worship. We'll discover why it's built the way it is and the reason for what may initially seem to be strange features.

But before we head inside, let's spend a moment longer in the yard. Why is it even worth going in? Do the content and style of a worship service really matter that much? Let me suggest that they do.

The Father's Quest

Just once in the Bible we're told the Father is looking for something. "The Son of Man [comes] to seek and to save the lost" (Luke 19:10). Christians are told to "seek first the kingdom of God" (Matt. 6:33). But the Father seeks only one thing: "True worshipers will worship the Father in spirit and truth, for the Father is seeking such people to worship him" (John 4:23). The Father is after worshippers. The Son of God—who was sent by his Father—knows this. To put it another way, Jesus was sent to rescue us so that we might worship.

Let that sink in. The Son of God took on flesh, became man, and dwelled among us so that we might worship. The Son of God walked in perfect obedience to his Father, fulfilling all righteousness and resisting the assaults of Satan, in order that we might worship. The Son of God was mocked, whipped, and spat at in order that we might worship. Saliva ran down the Creator's face in order that he might create worshippers. The Son of God was stripped and nailed to a cross. He suffered an agonizing death under the wrath of God in order that we might worship. The Son of God was torn apart, soul from body, buried in the ground before rising again, so that we might worship.

Does worship matter? Jesus clearly thinks so. The goal of the gospel is worship.

Reformation Recovery

Many of us are familiar with the Reformation, the great sixteenth-century movement to recover the grace of the gospel from the mire of medieval Roman Catholicism. What sometimes surprises people is how central the rediscovery of biblical worship was in the thinking of key Reformation leaders. For example, John Calvin wrote to Emperor Charles V that "the mode in which God is duly worshipped" takes the "*principal* place" in "the whole substance of Christianity," with "the source from which salvation is to be obtained" coming *second*.[1] How does the Christian faith get established and keep its place in society? Simple, says Calvin: You need to know two things—how to worship God and how to be saved. I'm pretty confident most of us would have skipped the worship point. We tend to think it's the gospel that matters; once you're saved, you can worship how you like. But Calvin understood that worship makes and shapes disciples.

The fact that worship shapes us is a key biblical principle. Take Psalm 115. Describing idols, the writer says,

> They have hands, but do not feel;
>   feet, but do not walk;
>   and they do not make a sound in their throat.
> Those who make them become like them;
>   so do all who trust in them. (vv. 7–8)

Idol worshippers become like their idols, because worship is formative and molds us into the image of whatever we revere. Thus the questions of who and how we worship are vital for the life and health of the church. In the pages that follow, we will see the great blessings of worshipping God in the manner he has laid out for us.

1

THE PROMISE OF WORSHIP

So, how should we worship? What are we meant to do? Once we see the importance of worship, these are natural questions for us to ask. But we need to slow down, at least a little. We've already seen that it is the Father who seeks worshippers, not the other way around. Worship begins not with our action but with God's. Before we can think about the right things to do in a worship service, we need to look at how God makes worship possible in the first place. Think of a game of tennis: you can't teach a player to return a serve unless someone else has served them a ball to begin with.

Worship, as we'll see, is like a conversation, a dialogue. But we're the second ones to speak, not the first. We won't know how to answer God in a way that pleases him until we see how he introduces himself and what he asks of us.

What's in a Word?

Already we're headed toward a tentative definition of *worship*. Worship is about what happens when God draws near to his people. As with many theological terms, there's no passage in Scripture where Jesus gives us a dictionary definition. Sometimes people start with the English word. *Worship* is derived from "worth-ship," giving the sense that to worship God is to declare his worth, his value, his excellence. This is no bad place to begin, as far as it goes. When we gather, that is part of what we do. But the Bible wasn't written in English!

Others turn to the various Hebrew and Greek words that tend to be translated as "worship" in English versions of the Bible. Here things get a bit trickier. For a start, several different words in both languages tend to end up as *worship* in our translations. To add even more confusion, those words are not *always* translated this way.

Take the Hebrew word *avad*. It appears in 2 Samuel 15:8, where Absalom promises, "If the LORD will indeed bring me back to Jerusalem, then I will offer worship to the LORD." Clearly Absalom is talking about going to the temple and worshipping in the direct sense of offering thanksgiving sacrifices. But the ESV translates *avad* as "work" when Adam is told to "work" and "keep" the ground (Gen. 2:15) and as "serve" when Moses and Pharaoh argue over who the people of Israel ought to serve (see Ex. 9:1; 14:5 among many others). These verses use the same Hebrew word to refer to general "all-of-life" worship rather than the temple-focused "worship service."

So to fix on one or two Greek or Hebrew words, examine their etymology as we did with "worth-ship," and come up with a definition of *worship* proves difficult. Some of these words have the sense of "to bow down"; others "to kiss"; others "to adore"; still others, as we've seen, "to work" or "to serve." Word studies have their place and can help to ensure we don't become too narrow in our understanding. But they're not enough to get us to where we want to be in terms of realizing what goes on when we gather each Sunday morning. So before trying to define *worship* any further, we need to return to the idea that worship is initiated by God.

Saved to Worship

Where to begin the story of worship? We might start at creation, looking up at the stars above. "The heavens declare the glory of God, and the sky above proclaims his handiwork" (Ps. 19:1). With Nehemiah we might look to the angels and say to God, "The host of heaven worships you" (Neh. 9:6). In fact we could look almost anywhere, as the great hymnbook of the Bible ends with the call, "Let everything that has breath praise the LORD!" (Ps. 150:6).

To cut to the chase, let's dive in to the story of the Exodus. God's people are enslaved to Pharaoh, but they are *God's* people. Not Pharaoh's. And so they need to be freed to worship him. Thankfully, God has made a commitment to them—a *covenant*, as the Bible calls it. *Covenant* is the Bible's word for God's relationship with his people. As the Israelites suffered under the Egyptian whip, "their cry for rescue from slavery came up to God. And God heard their groaning, and God remembered his covenant with Abraham, with Isaac, and with Jacob" (Ex. 2:23–24).

"God remembered" doesn't mean God was recalling something he'd forgotten. Rather, he was deciding to act on the basis of the covenant he had made. His remembering set off a battle between Pharaoh and God over whom Israel would serve. The battle most often is set out in terms of one of our worship words, *avad*. Sometimes the sense is what we might call *"all-of-life" worship* or, more simply, *service*. Hence the people of Israel "work [*avad*] as slaves" in Exodus 1:13, and later, after Israel is finally free, Pharaoh and his advisers have a change of heart, asking, "What is this we have done, that we have let Israel go from serving [*avad*] us?" (Ex. 14:5).

But the same word can be used for the more narrow sense of worship, the focused time of meeting with the Lord. Hence Yahweh promises Moses at the burning bush that "when you have brought the people out of Egypt, you shall serve [*avad*] God on this mountain" (Ex. 3:12). Here he isn't talking about an all-of-life posture but a focused time of worship. *Avad* is used plenty of other times in the Old Testament in this "narrow" sense of worship (see, for example, 2 Sam. 15:8; Ps. 102:22; Isa. 19:21).

At this point it's worth noticing that the idea of "all-of-life" worship doesn't come into being in the New Testament. Sometimes people have an understanding of worship that runs something like this: "In the Old Testament, Israel had to gather together to worship at the temple. But in the New Testament Jesus tells the Samaritan woman that people will no longer worship at the temple, but will worship in spirit and truth. This means that 'gathered worship' is replaced with 'all-of-life' worship. That's why Paul says we should offer our bodies as a living sacrifice, and this is our 'spiritual worship' (Rom. 12:1). Our gatherings nowadays are not about worship, because all of life is worship."

This line of reasoning would be as confusing to an Old Testament Israelite as it should be to a New Testament Christian! "What do you mean, 'All of life is now worship'?" the Israelite would say. "What do you think we've been doing for thousands of years?" Likewise, in John 4 Jesus isn't saying the idea of gathered worship is over: rather, the location is shifting. What was once focused on Jerusalem is going to be made possible worldwide for all who gather in the power of the Holy Spirit and truth of the gospel. Indeed, the whole conversation is precisely about gathered worship!

God's People: Assemble!

To return to Exodus, it is true that the great rescue enabled Israel to serve-worship Yahweh with all their lives. But the whole story drives toward a special meeting with God at Sinai. There God gathers his people and meets with them through his Word. They see nothing, but his voice thunders, often mediated through the prophet Moses. The

Word gathers the people to worship. From the first meeting at Mount Sinai onward, that day is known as "the day of assembly" (Deut. 9:10; 10:4; 18:16). God assembles his people to worship him by listening to his Word and making various offerings. The details we'll return to later. But a crucial principle is established: gathering to worship is a large part of the goal of God's rescue.

That's why when the Israelites leave Sinai, they don't leave behind the idea of a day of assembling to worship. In the fourth commandment, God gives his people a day of Sabbath rest, of ceasing from their daily work in order to gather to worship: "Six days shall work be done, but on the seventh day is a Sabbath of solemn rest, a holy convocation" (Lev. 23:3). *Convocation* isn't a word we use much nowadays, but it means a "calling together"—other translations, such as the New Living Translation, call it a "holy assembly." Later, the book of Psalms rings with calls for this assembly or congregation to praise and worship the Lord:

> Praise the LORD!
> I will give thanks to the LORD with my whole heart,
>   in the company of the upright, in the congregation.
>   (Ps. 111:1)

> Praise the LORD!
> Sing to the LORD a new song,
>   his praise in the assembly of the godly! (Ps. 149:1)

This understanding of the covenant-formed people of God meeting at his invitation, summoned by his Word, on the day of his choosing, in order to praise and worship him, is central to the whole Bible. It also gives us an insight into what worship is.

We could give all sorts of definitions that would be faithful to Scripture. From Psalm 29, we might say worship is gathering to proclaim God's greatness: "Ascribe to the LORD the glory due his name; worship the LORD in the splendor of holiness" (Ps. 29:2). From Psalm 95, we might focus on the idea of worship as a bowing before God: "Oh come, let us worship and bow down; let us kneel before the LORD, our Maker!" (Ps. 95:6). Others have focused on definitions of worship that boil down to lists of things to do: worship is singing, praying, preaching the Bible, and so on.

For a big-picture view, we might simply say that worship is the right response of God's people when they gather to meet him. One helpful book on worship has the great title *Engaging with God*.[1] The worship words, as we've seen, have breadth to them. Sometimes the focus *is* on a particular activity, like bowing down or singing. But every worship encounter is about God's meeting his people. For the purposes of this book, our focus will be on how that should look for the church as we gather each Lord's Day.

How Can We Worship?

Ask any Israelite where worship happens and they'd give you a simple answer. It happens, of course, at God's house, the temple or, in earlier form, the tabernacle. Where can you worship God other than the place of his presence? After all, to worship God, he needs to be there!

The Garden Temple

The first temple in the Bible isn't built with human hands. No, the first meeting place between God and man is the garden in Eden. Here God "walks in the cool of the day" (Gen. 3:8). In fact, the garden is described in very temple-like language. Or, rather, the tabernacle and temple that come later are depicted as miniature Edens. The temple curtain, guarding the way to the inner sanctum where God's footstool—the ark of the covenant—rested, had cherubim sewn into it. Why? Because the garden of Eden was guarded by cherubim. The candlestick in the Holy Place is shaped like a tree, and the temple is decorated with pomegranates and fruit, again to remind the worshipper of the original meeting place between God and his people. The tabernacle had to be set up with the entrance on the east, just as the garden had its entrance on the east (see Gen. 3:24).[2]

What's the significance of this? For those of us who are less steeped in the world of the Old Testament, it might pass us by, but for an Israelite reading Genesis 1–3 the implication would be clear. God built the garden in Eden as the first worship space and wanted to meet with his people. Our duty and our joy was meant to be found in worshipping and serving him. Already we're seeing a principle that will shape our own services: God decides where he will meet with his people. The invitation comes from him, and the location is therefore his to determine. We don't summon him where and when we see fit—the terms of engagement are his.

The Tabernacle Problem

Adam and Eve wanted more, though. Instead of worshipping and serving the Lord, they listened to Satan and were banished from paradise. Sin made them unfit for the presence of God, and thus the way back into his presence was guarded by the cherubim wielding a fiery sword. To try to approach God would mean death. Worship was now impossible.

And yet in his grace God didn't give up on his people. We've no space here to explore every stage on the journey, but throughout the book of Genesis we meet those who call on the name of the Lord, a people who are somehow able to worship. Sometimes they bring offerings like Abel; sometimes they build altars like Abraham. But events take a huge leap forward with the rescuing of Israel from Egypt and the building of the tabernacle.

The book of Exodus ends with God "moving in" to his new earthly home. Of course, in one sense he is always present everywhere. But it's at the center of the tabernacle that the glory cloud, the visible symbol of God's special presence, settles. God is back dwelling with his people. Yet a problem remains. God has commanded Moses, "On the first day of the first month you shall erect the *tabernacle* of the *tent of meeting*" (Ex. 40:2).

The tent has two names. It is first a tabernacle, a "dwelling place" for God. But it's also meant to be "tent of meeting." Two different Hebrew words describe the same physical entity. By the end of Exodus, the tent is certainly a dwelling place. But God's moving in means everyone else has to move out:

> Then the cloud covered the tent of meeting, and the glory of the LORD filled the tabernacle. And Moses was not able to enter the tent of meeting because the cloud settled on it, and the glory of the LORD filled the tabernacle. (Ex. 40:34–35)

Even Moses can't remain in the tent when God's presence arrives. So, says Old Testament scholar Michael Morales, the tabernacle (dwelling place) isn't yet a meeting place.[3] No sinner can draw near. Worship is still an impossibility.

Through Fire and Sword

Thankfully the Bible doesn't end with Exodus. The very next book, Leviticus, begins,

> The LORD called Moses and spoke to him from the tent of meeting, saying, "Speak to the people of Israel and

say to them, When any one of you brings an offering to the LORD, you shall bring your offering of livestock from the herd or from the flock." (Lev. 1:1–2)

God is active, calling Moses to come before him. And again, God is seeking worshippers to draw near. You could translate God's words in verse 2 "If any man [*adam* in Hebrew] draws near . . ." God is making a way for man—Adam!—to return to his presence. And as the rest of the book of Leviticus makes clear, this requires sacrifices or offerings. In fact, the word translated *offering* in Leviticus comes from the Hebrew word meaning "draw near." We might say the Israelites are to draw near with their "draw-nearings"! These offerings of various animals allow the worshipper to safely approach the Lord.

Although there's considerable variety in the five main offerings Leviticus details, at the core is the idea that an animal must be killed and then burned on the altar before any further worship can take place. Notice that the animal, which stands in place of the worshipper, must pass through sword and fire—it must be killed by the blade, then burned on the altar. It's as if the cherubim's fiery sword falls on the lamb instead of Adam. Once that has taken place, and the worshipper is "clean" in God's sight, then a whole host of other offerings and festivities can begin. And there were plenty of them! The Israelite calendar, be it the week, month, or year, was structured around the worship of God. But no offerings or festivities could take place until sword and fire had consumed the sin-bearing substitute for the worshipper.

Leviticus and the whole tabernacle system reaffirm the lesson of Eden: it is God who decides where he meets his people. They also begin to make clear that it is God who decides *how* we may approach.

The Fire and Sword of Golgotha

At this stage you might be forgiven for wondering if you've been shortchanged. Wasn't this meant to be a book on worship, not a study guide to Leviticus? But what we're beginning to see, I hope, is that the story of the Bible is the story of worship. Created to meet in joyful awe of God, at the place and time of his choosing, right at the beginning we instead turned aside to worship other "gods." The just response of God was to expel us from paradise and leave us under threat of fire and sword if we dared draw near. And yet his grace continued to shine through: the Old Testament sacrificial system provided a way that his people could meet with him to worship, albeit in a limited way. The tabernacle shows it's no small thing for a person to wander into God's presence—but it was perhaps going to be possible again. The sacrifices are not an end in themselves: they are the prerequisite to drawing near to God in worship.

Yet as the book of Hebrews makes clear, what is required for our full restoration to the presence of God is not an animal substitute but a human one. The Son of

God came in the flesh, made like us in every way, in order that he might carry our sin to the cross and there bear the righteous anger of God in our place. Jesus went under the fire and sword in order that we might be spared. Death and judgment consumed him in order that they might never consume his people. He is the "Lamb of God, who takes away the sin of the world" (John 1:29).

Like the old covenant sacrifices that pictured his work, Jesus's once-and-for-all sacrifice had a purpose. The death of Christ makes us able to enter God's presence again, to draw near in humble confidence. This is a repeated theme of Hebrews:

> Let us then with confidence *draw near* to the throne of grace, that we may receive mercy and find grace to help in time of need. (Heb. 4:16)

> On the other hand, a better hope is introduced, through which we *draw near* to God. (Heb. 7:19)

> Consequently, he is able to save to the uttermost those who *draw near* to God through him. (Heb. 7:25)

> Let us *draw near* with a true heart in full assurance of faith, with our hearts sprinkled clean from an evil conscience and our bodies washed with pure water. (Heb. 10:22)

Remember that Leviticus began with God's instructing Moses on how he might draw near. Here at last in the atoning death of Jesus is the answer.

There's plenty we might say about what the cross achieves. But for our purposes we'll focus on one theme: the cross makes worship possible. Think of Jesus's cry as darkness enveloped him at Golgotha. "My God, my God, why have you forsaken me?" He was quoting the first line of Psalm 22. If you take a moment to read that psalm, you'll see it's an incredible prophecy of the crucifixion. The first twenty-one verses walk in painstaking detail through the agony of the cross, the descent of Christ to death. But the psalm doesn't end there. Verse 22 is a turning point, a transition from death to life:

> I will tell of your name to my brothers;
>> in the midst of the congregation I will praise you:
> You who fear the LORD, praise him!
>> All you offspring of Jacob, glorify him,
>> and stand in awe of him, all you offspring of Israel!
>>> (vv. 22–23)

The One who went down to death has now returned! And why? To lead the congregation in worship. (Notice the assembly or congregation theme again!) We'll return to this idea at various points in the coming chapters, but for now just notice that the very psalm that Jesus uses to give us a glimpse into what's going on at Calvary is the same psalm that prophesies that the Crucified One will rise again to lead his people in worship. Worship is the goal of atonement.

The Ultimate Worship Leader

All this means that worship is ultimately led by Jesus. He is the one who makes it safe for sinners like us to approach God. Jesus is the Christ or Messiah. These words—one Greek, one Hebrew—mean the same thing: *anointed*. In the Old Testament, three types of people were anointed by having oil poured on their heads as a sign of their commissioning as servants of God. These three were the prophets, priests, and kings. Jesus inherits each of their mantles. As *prophet*, he is the one through whom God speaks to us. As *king*, he rules over us and defends us. As *priest*, he atones for our sin and intercedes for us. All three roles have relevance for our worship. It is Jesus the prophet who speaks to us when his Word is faithfully preached. It is Jesus the king who determines what the people are and aren't to do as we gather together. And it is Jesus the priest who leads the congregation in worship.

All this means there is no way to meet God other than in and through Christ. He is not only our Great High Priest (see Heb. 4:14); he is the true temple where God and man meet (see John 2:21). So if you want to meet God, see his glory, and worship, the only place to come is to Jesus.

The People Who Worship

If Jesus is both the leader and place of worship, then we can already answer the question "Who can worship?" The answer is anyone who has put their trust in him. True worship is possible only for Christians. No one else can approach God in safety; no one else can be accepted. Jesus is the only truly beloved Son of heaven, he is the only high priest, he is the only atoning sacrifice. And he is therefore the only worship leader. Only those who bear his name worship with him. To return to Psalm 22 (picked up and applied to Jesus in Hebrews 2), Christ promises God that he will "tell of your name to *my brothers*" (Ps. 22:22). It is Christ's family who gathers to worship; worship is for the church.

This has significance for how we think of our services. They are not *primarily* evangelistic events. We are not called to plan them *primarily* for those outside the church. Mission-minded pastors and Christians are sometimes tempted to try to remove everything from worship that might either offend or confuse a non-Christian. Often this is done with the best of motives as they try to create a place for non-Christians to hear the gospel. And of course it's wonderful if unbelievers and seekers come along on Sunday mornings. Paul envisages just such a circumstance in 1 Corinthians 14:24–26.

But when friends come along to a worship service, they are being invited to see the church doing what she is called to do: worship the living God. They won't be helped if we hide away large chunks of who we are and what God has called us to do. Rather than trying to be novel and relevant, we find real freedom and power in trusting God to work in the ways he has given. Our friends will hear Jesus speak through his Word. They'll see his people pouring out their concerns and cares on a Good Shepherd who loves them. They'll listen as the comfort and assurance of the gospel is applied to wounded sheep. In short, they'll get to watch as God meets with his people during the most significant hour of the week. And we pray that, like the man in 1 Corinthians 14, they might "fall down and worship God, exclaiming, 'God is really among you!'" (v. 25 NIV).

But all this comes about as the church gathers in Jesus's name and worships as he instructs us, not as we eradicate prayers, shorten sermons to five-minute TED Talks, pepper the service with film clips, and serve donuts and coffee halfway through. We can trust God's gifts to achieve God's purposes!

Conclusion

Worship is all about meeting with God through Christ. Rather than thinking of it as an activity we perform, either to keep God happy or to keep one another going, our first thoughts should go to God and to his grace and mercy. That he desires to meet with us is extraordinary! Already we can see that, whatever we say about what we do in worship, these activities are not ladders we climb to get closer to God. Rather they are "means of grace"—things God uses to bless his people.

Questions for Further Reflection

1. How would you describe the link between the gospel and worship?
2. What is happening when the church gathers to worship?
3. What would you say to someone who says, "All of life is worship, so there's nothing special about gathering together on a Sunday"?
4. What is the significance of Jesus being our worship leader?
5. Read again the "draw near" verses from Hebrews on page 31. What things can hinder us from wanting to draw near? How does the gospel encourage us to do so?

2

THE PURPOSE OF WORSHIP

Most Christians will admit there are Sunday mornings when they awaken and wonder whether it's even worth getting out of bed. Surely God doesn't need our worship? We're not serving on the setup team this week. No one will notice if we're not there. We can perhaps read the Bible ourselves a bit later, pray from the comfort of the couch, pop on some Christian music over coffee. So why bother with corporate worship?

The answer is found not so much by searching the Scriptures for commands to gather—though those commands are certainly there. Rather, we need to look at the God who calls us to worship. I didn't marry my wife because someone explained the duties and responsibilities of a husband—though those responsibilities are clearly presented in the Bible. No, I met, got to know, and fell in love with Georgina. So we'll focus on just two truths about God that help us to understand why we worship and what blessings come as a result.

The God Who Deserves Everything

Creatures are made to worship their Creator. When anyone, be they human or angel, turns to think about who God is and what he's done, the right response is worship.

Unlike bleary-eyed Christians on a Sunday morning, those already in heaven see God clearly and react instinctively to encountering him. To give just one example, in Revelation 4 we meet four strange creatures who live before the throne of God. What do they spend their lives doing? "Day and night they never cease to say, 'Holy, holy, holy, is the Lord God Almighty, who was and is and is to come!'" (Rev. 4:8). These heavenly beings spend every moment in worship: it's as if it never occurs to them to do anything else. Here they praise God for who he is. He is holy, he is all-powerful, he is eternal. Seeing God's character and attributes leads to an outburst of praise.

It's the same when the twenty-four elders, perhaps symbolic of the redeemed people of God, respond to the creatures' song: "Worthy are you, our Lord and God, to receive glory and honor and power, for you created all things, and by your will they existed and were created" (Rev. 4:11). This time the focus is not so much on who God is but on what he has done: he has created all things and sustains them moment by moment. Regularly in Scripture, worship emerges from a worshipper's reflections on the wonderful deeds of God. The Psalms are full of this pattern. Take Psalm 147, which begins with the classic exhortation "Praise the LORD!" The whole psalm then piles up reasons to praise him.

> The LORD builds up Jerusalem;
>> he gathers the outcasts of Israel.
> He heals the brokenhearted
>> and binds up their wounds.
> He determines the number of the stars;
>> he gives to all of them their names. (Ps. 147:2–4)

As the psalmist reflects on God's kindness to his people—his building of the church and his willingness to deal tenderly with the brokenhearted, even as he is also the one who flung stars into space—he can't help but worship.

In the New Testament era, it's no different. As we return to the heavenly throne room, we meet the elders and creatures who are combining their voices to praise Jesus for all he's done: "Worthy is the Lamb who was slain, to receive power and wealth and wisdom and might and honor and glory and blessing!" (Rev. 5:12).

We could multiply examples almost endlessly. Worship ultimately is what we do when we draw near to God. It is his due. Everything we are and have comes from him, so it's right that we respond in humble thanks and praise.

The Joy of Worship

But we mustn't think this is mere duty, the kind of reverence shown by terrified citizens who are called to bow before the image of a despotic dictator. Rather, to worship God is our greatest privilege and joy. Perhaps the most famous lines ever to come from a Presbyterian pen are the question and answer that open the Westminster Shorter Catechism: "What is the chief end of man? Man's chief end is to glorify God and enjoy him forever." Glorifying God is not a separate activity from enjoying him forever. Notice the question isn't "What are the *two* chief ends of man?" but what is our one, singular "end" or purpose. Incredible though it may seem, God has created us for joy—to share with us the greatest gift he could give: himself. And the way we experience that delight is by worshipping him. This is why the Psalms are so full of joy.

> In your presence there is fullness of joy;
> at your right hand are pleasures forevermore.
>   (Ps. 16:11)

> Then I will go to the altar of God,
>   to God my exceeding joy,
> and I will praise you with the lyre,
>   O God, my God. (Ps. 43:4)

With joy and gladness they are led along
as they enter the palace of the king. (Ps. 45:15)

Worship is not just a duty but a delight. We are built to worship, to give ourselves in wonder to something—or rather Someone—who is awesome and worthy. In fact, in the Bible's understanding everyone is a worshipper. The question isn't *whether* we'll worship but *who* we'll worship. In Romans 1, Paul's critique of humanity isn't that they stopped worshipping but rather that "they exchanged the truth about God for a lie and worshiped and served the creature rather than the Creator" (Rom. 1:25). Stop worshipping God and we'll start worshipping something else. To put it another way, every human being on earth will be worshipping next Sunday morning. The only question is who or what they'll worship: the triune God or Allah, Baal, comfort, golf, family, or any of the thousands of other idols we give ourselves to. And from what we've seen already, this switch is not just evil but foolish. It's to swap pure spring water for filthy sewage, a king's banquet for rat poison and arsenic.

God deserves everything; he deserves *all* our worship.

The God Who Needs Nothing

So we worship God because he deserves everything, and in that worship we know the blessing of joy and wonder as we meet him. But there's another truth about God that at first sight might seem strange but that turns out to be a tremendous encouragement as Sunday morning rolls around. That strangely good news is that God doesn't need us. More than that, in fact: God doesn't need *anything*.

This is sometimes known as God's self-sufficiency or independence. It emerges from the first verse of the Bible, where we learn that God created the heavens and earth. The sky, the stars, the earth we stand on: it all depends on God, the uncreated one, for its existence. Human beings rely on fuel to run; we need water, air, and food to sustain us. God, however, needs nothing. He is entirely self-existent. That's why he reveals himself to Moses at the burning bush as "I AM" (Ex. 3:14). Though the fire (which represents God) is in the bush, the bush isn't actually burning—the fire needs no fuel.

Because God made all things and owns all things and is himself dependent on nothing, it's ultimately impossible for anyone to really give anything to him—at least in the sense of giving so he genuinely gains from it. Paul makes exactly this point.

> "Or who has given a gift to him
> that he might be repaid?"

> For from him and through him and to him are all things.
> To him be glory forever. Amen. (Rom. 11:35–36)

The answer to Paul's question is clearly "No one." No one has ever given anything to God, putting God in their debt. Why not? Because everything came from him, exists because of him, and is made for him. What could you give him that isn't his already? What can you add to benefit an all-knowing, all-powerful, eternally happy God?

The self-sufficiency of God has huge implications for our understanding of worship. When we gather on a Sunday, who is gaining? Not God, but us. We don't come because he needs us but because we need him. We come ultimately not to give but to gain. How else could needy, dependent sinners approach the God of all life? As Paul writes to the Athenians,

> The God who made the world and everything in it, being Lord of heaven and earth, does not live in temples made by man, nor is he served by human hands, as though he needed anything, since he himself gives to all mankind life and breath and everything. (Acts 17:24–25)

This truth about God helps to shed even more light on the worship service in heaven we saw earlier. There we heard that God was worthy to receive "glory and honor and power" (Rev. 4:11). But what does it mean for God to "receive" glory from his people? The self-sufficiency of God shows us that it can't mean God is actually becoming more glorious. His glory is already infinite! Likewise, as he is praised, he doesn't become more powerful. Rather, the elders' song declares that all the praise, all the honor, all the power used by creatures in worship ought to be directed solely to God. It is right that we worship him with all that we are and all that we have—in that sense we give him glory. But as we do so, he isn't gaining; incredibly, we are.

C. S. Lewis gives a good illustration of this principle, which is worth quoting at length.

> Every faculty you have, your power of thinking or of moving your limbs from moment to moment, is given you by God. If you devoted every moment of your whole life exclusively to His service you could not give Him anything that was not in a sense His own already. So that when we talk of a man doing anything for God or giving anything to God, I will tell you what it is really like. It is like a small child going to [his or her] father and saying, "Daddy, give me sixpence to buy you a birthday present." Of course, the father does, and he is pleased with the child's present. It is all very nice and proper, but only an idiot would think that the father is sixpence to the good on the transaction.[1]

When we sing to God, pray to him, and give of our money, he remains sixpence none the richer. But we, doing what we were created for, are immeasurably blessed. The glory is his, the gain ours.

The Grace of Worship

All this is really another way of saying that our ability to come to worship is an act of grace on God's part. He who has everything graciously and freely shares with his needy people. When we grasp that God needs nothing from us, we can see even more clearly that all he gives us comes from his self-giving love.

In any human relationship, there is always an element of gain for both parties. In a healthy marriage, each spouse focuses on serving the other's needs. But no honest husband or wife would claim they've never received any blessing back themselves. The reason we married in the first place is likely because we wanted to spend life with a person we found interesting or beautiful or comforting or fun or . . . Whatever the reason, both parties went down the aisle knowing they were gaining immeasurably. Not so God. He does nothing but give—a sure sign that his love is entirely unconditioned on us. He gives freely in Christ, needing nothing, not seeking to take from us but instead to bless.

This is a huge encouragement for us to come to worship, perhaps especially when we don't feel especially "spiritual." We can come to God honestly—broken, sinful, struggling, doubting—knowing that we won't be turned away if we come in the name of his Son. We need his help, his mercy, his strength. We need our sins to be forgiven, our souls revived. All this and more God can do for us when we meet with him. And because he needs nothing, we don't need to sort ourselves out before coming to him. Rather, we put our faith in Jesus as our Savior and Mediator and, by faith alone, approach the throne of grace.

This, after all, is the gospel. Christ came for sinners. He who was rich made himself nothing, humbling himself to death on the cross. And all for our sake. He need not have left heaven; he need not have rescued us. That he did shows God's incalculably gracious love.

Martin Luther wrote a beautiful prayer that captures these themes of God's self-sufficiency and our need:

> In you I have sealed the treasure of all I have.
> I am poor; you are rich and came to be merciful to
>   the poor.
> I am a sinner; you are upright.
> With me, there is an abundance of sin; in you is the
>   fullness of righteousness.
> Therefore I will remain with you, of whom I can
>   receive, but to whom I may not give.
> Amen.[2]

How do you approach a God who needs nothing? As a beggar.

The Tone of Worship

Perhaps this is a good place to pause and reflect on what we might call the *tone* of worship. What should services feel like? Perhaps you've started attending a Reformed church and it seems more formal than you'd expected. Less fun, even. What's going on?

How we behave is hugely shaped by where we are. We act one way at a wedding, another way at a funeral. We know how to behave in a hospital, a café, and a school. So how should we behave when we gather with God's people on the day he appointed for us to meet with him?

Well, where are we? Because of all we saw in the last chapter about God's bringing-near work in Christ, Christians are those who are, spiritually speaking, already safely home before God's throne. Paul tells the Ephesians that God has "seated us with him in the heavenly places in Christ Jesus" (Eph. 2:6). Even as we live out our lives in our earthly villages, towns, and cities, we are at the same time "in Christ" and therefore mysteriously present before the Lord.

The author of the book of Hebrews makes the comparison between the gathering at Mount Sinai—where God's people had to keep their distance for fear of being consumed by the holiness of God—and new covenant worship. But having reassured the Hebrew Christians that they are not at Mount Sinai, the writer doesn't tell them that they've not come to a mountain at all. Rather, it is on a different mountain that we now approach God, in a different gathering:

> But you have come to Mount Zion and to the city of the living God, the heavenly Jerusalem, and to

> innumerable angels in festal gathering, and to the
> assembly of the firstborn who are enrolled in heaven,
> and to God, the judge of all, and to the spirits of the
> righteous made perfect, and to Jesus, the mediator of a
> new covenant, and to the sprinkled blood that speaks
> a better word than the blood of Abel. (Heb. 12:22–24)

Because of the gospel, Christians are constantly in the presence of the Lord, but that presence is intensified when we assemble to worship and God draws near through his appointed means. As we gather to worship, it's as if we're walking not just into a church sanctuary or rented gym but into the very halls of heaven.

I sometimes ask the children at our church where we're meeting today. By now they're wise to the trick. The answer is both "Leeds, a city in the north of England" and, more importantly, "heaven." Similarly, when I ask who we're meeting with, the answer is twofold. With our earthly eyes, we see Pastor Reuben inviting us to stand and sing, Professor Jeff and his wife Caroline marshalling their troupe of kids, Davey the professional track runner and his adoring little brother Jonny. But with the eyes of faith, we see more: There are the angels Gabriel and Michael, leading a throng of angels we can't begin to count. There are all the believers who have died and gone before us, including many we've known and loved ourselves. And there is Jesus, leading his brothers and sisters in worship before God's throne.

When we remember where we are and who we're with, the tone of worship begins to fall into place. In fact, the Hebrews passage spells it out for us: "Let us offer to God acceptable worship, with reverence and awe, for our God is a consuming fire" (Heb. 12:28–29). We have not come to a theater to be entertained and amused. Nor have we come to a school to be educated. Sometimes those from churches with a clearer focus on Bible teaching are dismissive of churches they think are simply fixated on entertainment. But it's perfectly possible that "learning the main theme of Ephesians 1" can become a university-educated person's form of entertainment: "edutainment," to borrow a phrase from John Jefferson Davis.[3] Rather, we have come to God's throne room to meet the Lord, and the "tone" flows from there.

Again the Psalms help to guide us, not least because they are the Spirit-written prayer book of the church. As we saw earlier, joy is everywhere. While we are refreshed again in the grace of God, renewed in his strength, and reminded of his unfathomable love, we pray the Spirit would enable us to rejoice before the Lord. In Psalm 2, we learn that we are to "serve the LORD with fear and rejoice with trembling" (v. 11). To "rejoice with trembling" while also "fearing" the Lord could seem almost contradictory to us. Our culture too quickly associates joy with casualness, frivolity, silliness. When you come to the God who deserves everything but needs nothing, the God who is "holy, holy, holy" yet has freely loved and forgiven sinners, joy and reverent fear suddenly seem to be a natural combination.

So when you read of the great worship encounters of the Bible—perhaps the gathering at Sinai or, even more pertinently, the heavenly worship scenes—you don't get the impression that the congregation is stopping for donut breaks or to watch a funny clip from the latest sitcom to help them engage. Rather, they are focused on God in his grace and glory, and the tone of worship flows from that. If you would be embarrassed to be doing whatever you're doing if Gabriel and the archangel Michael turned up, the chances are things have gone awry somewhere.

Hence the pastor's job in planning and leading a service—and the congregation member's goal in participating in worship—is not to entertain or even just to educate. Nor is it to chase an experience, but rather it is to encounter God. The "experience" flows from that encounter, and it will take different shapes at different times of life.

In other words, once you start to search for joy, awe, comfort, or any other emotion in worship, you've already headed down the wrong path. This is, in fact, a great relief: there will be plenty of times when we don't feel particularly happy, for example. The tragedies of life mean that real saints may well be weeping through a worship service. But we can still come and meet with our God, the great Shepherd, in reverent awe.

So, come Sunday morning, must you go to worship? Yes, but it's not that sort of *must*. It's the *must* of "You must eat this roast dinner" or "You must kiss your spouse." It may even feel at times like the *must* of "Son, you must drink this medicine." But, on the basis of God's promise, by faith we know we are doing something that is not just right but also good. In his incredible mercy, God has tied our duty to our delight. As we give him everything, we lose nothing and gain more than we could begin to imagine.

Questions for Further Reflection

1. How does the idea that God deserves everything change how we approach worship?
2. How does the idea that God needs nothing change how we approach worship?
3. How would you help a new Christian who asks why we worship?
4. What "tone" do you think worship should have Sunday by Sunday? Why?

3

THE PRINCIPLE OF WORSHIP

From all we've seen so far, I hope it has become clear that God is the primary actor in worship. He sought us out, when we were lost in sin, to establish a covenant relationship with us. We didn't find our way back to him or devise our own plan of salvation to initiate that covenant relationship. Now, as we turn to consider *how* the church should worship, we'll see that this dynamic continues. God begins the covenant, and he decides what shape that relationship takes as it continues. He sets the terms. This is great news! Far from having to think up creative new ideas week by week to keep God's people entertained or hope that what we dream up might perhaps be pleasing to him, we can simply do the things he has told us to do. To put it another way, God cares not just whom we worship but how we worship.

This, for many Christians, comes as something of a surprise. So let's dive back into Scripture to see how the principle is established.

Strange Fire

We'll begin once again in the days of the tabernacle. Remember, though, that although we're dealing with the old covenant, and therefore with an era that has passed away, God himself has not changed. Although we don't worship in exactly the same manner as an Old Testament believer, sacrificing goats and baking bread offerings, we are approaching the same God. And that God cares about how we approach.

Leviticus begins by making exactly that point. God calls Moses and says to him, "Speak to the people of Israel and say to them, When any one of you brings an offering to the LORD, you shall bring . . ." (Lev. 1:2). What follows is seven chapters with detailed description of what the various offerings should look like. The Israelites aren't invited to bring whatever comes to hand. God prescribes which animals are to be offered in which circumstances. He makes rules about who does what and where. He describe what the animals that are offered are to be like. He gives directions on the order the various offerings are to be made in and what should happen to any remains. And that's not even counting the last fifteen chapters of Exodus, which lay out the pattern for the tabernacle and dress code for the priests, or the rest of the book of Leviticus, which goes on to institute various holy days, festivals, and feasts. Everything is specified by God in his Word.

This is made particularly clear with the first great "worship service" in the tabernacle. Take a moment to cast your eyes over Leviticus 8 and 9. Even if you don't follow every detail, you'll perhaps notice a repeated theme. Time and again we read that everything was done "as the LORD commanded Moses" (Lev. 8:4, 9, 13, 17, and so on!). Here is a worship service that is ordered according to God's Word. Moses and Aaron don't try to innovate or add to God's patterns and plans. Rather, they do exactly as he has commanded. And the result? God accepts their offerings and worship, and the people fall down in joyful worship. God consumed the sacrifice—but not them (see Lev. 9:24)!

The whole day has been a roaring success. Perhaps it's the joy of the people that encourages Aaron's sons, who've recently been consecrated to be priests along with him, to get creative. We don't know exactly what they did. But we do know exactly what they didn't do: worship God according to his Word. Straight after the joyful climax of Leviticus 9, we read, "Now Nadab and Abihu, the sons of Aaron, each took his censer and put fire in it and laid incense on it and offered unauthorized fire before the LORD, which he had not commanded them" (Lev. 10:1).

The boys have decided to spice things up. Perhaps repeating the things that worked last time seemed boring to them. Perhaps they thought God wouldn't care how they worshipped. Perhaps they wanted to build up their own followers, a gang who preferred their worship style to that of Dad and Uncle Moses. Who knows? The text doesn't say. What is crystal clear is that this offering was "unauthorized," a style of worship that God "had not commanded them." The result is devastating: "Fire came out from before the LORD and consumed them, and they died before the LORD" (Lev. 10:2). Instead of the sacrifice, they were consumed. Unlike the worship service in Leviticus 9, which ends with joyful, exuberant shouting, Leviticus 10's worship service ends in deathly silence: "Aaron held his peace" (v. 3).

Some people want to apply this passage just to the question of how we get saved. "We mustn't try to approach God in any way other than the one he commands: in the gospel of Christ." This, of course, is true—a vital point! But I'm not sure it's all the passage has to say. After all, Nadab and Abihu weren't Egyptians trying to "get saved." No, they were members of God's people trying to approach him in worship. Indeed, the whole tabernacle system was one of worship, not primarily salvation.

It's tempting to think that the Old Testament sacrifices worked like the Roman Catholic confessional—or at least a popular perception of it. In this view, Joe the Israelite sins and knows he needs forgiveness. Off he goes to collect his best goat, head to the tabernacle, confess his sin, lay hands on the animal, and offer the sacrifice. Bingo! He's forgiven and back to being saved and on his way to heaven. But then—disaster! On his way home, he sees his old enemy Zebediah, and the two fall into a scuffle. Joe, aware that he's sinned, rushes home, grabs the next goat, and heads back to the tabernacle. Phew! Just in time, he sacrifices again, is forgiven again, saved again. Then, just as he's nearly home, he catches sight of Zebediah's beautiful wife. Joe's third best goat begins to tremble . . .

No. The sacrifices picture Christ and his once-and-for-all offering—large sections of Hebrews are taken up with exactly that idea. But a believing Israelite trusted in the same once-and-for-all gospel as we do. He may have known less, since he lived at an earlier stage of God's plan. But like us he was saved through faith in God's gospel promise—saved indeed by Christ! In the books of Romans and Galatians, Paul regularly goes back to Abraham to show that believers have always been justified—declared righteous before God—through faith alone. Offering sacrifices wasn't chiefly about getting saved, initiating the covenant relationship. No, the tabernacle, and later the temple, system was about the ongoing relationship. That's why Hebrews calls those who brought offerings "worshipers" (Heb. 9:9; 10:2) and the whole system one of "worship" (Heb. 9:21).

Which brings us back to Nadab and Abihu. Their story teaches us that God cares about being worshipped according to his Word. It is possible, but not at all wise, to worship the right God in the wrong way.[1]

The Invisible Word

This brings us to another key text: the Ten Commandments. The first commandment is clear and well known:

"You shall have no other gods before me" (Deut. 5:7). The third, about bearing God's name in vain, sometimes causes a bit of head-scratching, but by commandment four and the Sabbath, we're away. No murder, adultery, theft . . . all perfectly clear.

But what about the second commandment? Here's how it begins: "You shall not make for yourself a carved image, or any likeness of anything that is in heaven above, or that is on the earth beneath, or that is in the water under the earth" (Deut. 5:8). What is this adding to the first? There's overlap, certainly. God's people are not to make images of any created thing or false god and bow down to them in worship. But the commandment goes further.

Deuteronomy 4 helps to clarify. Moses reminds the people of the first great "day of assembly," when they gathered at Mount Sinai. There, "the LORD spoke to you out of the midst of the fire. You heard the sound of words, but saw no form; there was only a voice" (Deut. 4:12). No form, just words. Moses draws out the significance:

> Therefore watch yourselves very carefully. Since you saw no form on the day that the LORD spoke to you at Horeb out of the midst of the fire, beware lest you act corruptly by making a carved image for yourselves, in the form of any figure, the likeness of male or female, the likeness of any animal that is on the earth, the likeness of any winged bird that flies in the air, the likeness of anything that creeps on the ground, the likeness of

any fish that is in the water under the earth. (Deut. 4:15–18)

Do you see the link? You didn't see God, you just heard him. Therefore, don't make any images. Of course that means no making images of Baal, Zeus, or Vishnu to worship. But out of order too are images of God, be they in human, animal, bird, or fish form. It is not OK to worship the invisible God using visible images. The second commandment moves on from the "Who?" of worship to the "How?"

It is this commandment that the Israelites so brazenly broke with the golden calf. It's not hard to imagine the circumstances. Moses had been out of sight, up in the clouds of the mountains for days. God and his appointed mediator seemed distant. The people didn't want to rely on the words they'd heard; they wanted something more tangible, something more "real," something to bring God closer. Hence the golden calf. "It's not idolatry!" they might protest. "We're worshipping Yahweh! It's just we're worshipping him in a way that feels more real to us."

But God has spoken: worship is to be directed by his Word, not our will. This is the principle that comes thundering into the new covenant. We let God's Word direct our worship. Yes, God is invisible. Yes, for now, the one true Mediator, Jesus Christ, has, like Moses, gone up out of sight. We, like Israel, may feel the pressure to innovate, to "bring him closer," in ways that seem fitting to us. But this is neither honoring to God nor beneficial to his people.

A Principle That's Passed?

It's often pointed out that there is no "New Testament Leviticus." So, the reasoning goes, it must be OK to worship God in any way we see fit, provided there's nothing sinful about it. We're all agreed there's no more sacrificing goats or proceeding to Jerusalem each year for Passover. Similarly, all Christians are agreed that *some* things would be inappropriate in worship. X-rated movies, drunken parties, invoking the names of other "gods" are all clearly off-limits. But as long as it isn't forbidden, does more or less anything go in worship?

Reformed Christians have argued no. The principles established in the Old Testament—that God cares how he is worshipped and that his Word directs what that worship should look like—haven't been abolished in the new covenant. For starters, none of the other nine commandments have been revoked, so why should the second? Likewise, God himself hasn't changed, so why would he be concerned with how he was approached in the old covenant but not at all in the new?

So yes, it's true that new covenant worship is simpler and, in a sense, "easier" than old covenant worship. There is no New Testament Leviticus with precise directions for worship. Nor have New Testament feasts and festivals been instituted to replace the Passover, Feast of Booths, and Feast of Weeks.

But at the same time it's vital that we don't read the New Testament as if it has dropped fresh from heaven, unconnected to what came before. Instead, we should read it as a continuation of all that's come before. It's virtually impossible to understand most of the New without a rich understanding of the Old. And some things are taken for granted in the (much shorter) New Testament, on the assumption that we've learned them in the Old.

Take, for example, the question of who we can marry. The Gospels and Epistles say little to nothing about it. So could you marry your sister or aunt? Of course not! This would fall under the category of "sexual immorality," says the "New Testament only" believer. And they're right! But wait a minute—how do you know it's immoral to marry your aunt but OK to marry your cousin?[2] We have to read the Old Testament and take note of its moral laws—the laws that don't change over time. Thus we turn up to the New Testament, having read the Old, with a host of principles in place. Often we see only echoes of them in the New, since it expects us to fill out the picture with all we've learned from the Old. They are *together* the Scriptures, after all!

We therefore arrive at the New Testament with various expectations about worship. We're not surprised to see that Paul was concerned about what happens when the church gathers. To the Corinthians he gives instructions about, among other things, who may speak (see 1 Cor. 14:34–35), how worshippers should dress (see 1 Cor. 11:4–16), how many prophets may prophesy (see 1 Cor. 14:27–33), and what should happen if someone prophesies in a foreign language (see 1 Cor. 14:1–25). He is absolutely not happy for worship to be a free-for-all as the Corinthians worship as they want! All these instructions have to do with the "gathered worship" of the church. They are about when the church "comes together" (1 Cor. 11:17–18, 20, 33–34; 14:23, 26). They by no means apply to "all-of-life" worship: otherwise Paul would be forbidding women to ever speak (see 1 Cor. 14:34)!

Then there's the church in Colossae. Here Paul's concern is that the church has drifted away from the sufficiency of Jesus and the Word that brings him to us. What he wants is for them to "let the word of Christ dwell in you richly, teaching and admonishing one another in all wisdom, singing psalms and hymns and spiritual songs, with thankfulness in your hearts to God" (Col. 3:16). Instead they are turning aside to all sorts of other innovations in worship, including visions, ascetic practices, and even the worship of angels. All these are man-made practices—diversions from and additions to the Word of God (see Col. 3:16–23).

Worship is never a free-for-all. We come to a God who continues to care how he's worshipped.

The Freedom of Word Worship

We'll return later to think much more about what new covenant worship should look like. But I hope what we've seen so far has established the principle: worship is to be governed by God's Word. We do in worship what

God tells us to do. And we don't do things he hasn't told us to!

This idea is sometimes known as the *regulative principle*. It's a principle embedded in most of the Reformed confessions of faith, albeit phrased in somewhat different ways.[3] Here, for example, is how the Westminster Confession of Faith puts it: "The acceptable way of worshipping the true God is instituted by himself, and so limited to his own revealed will, that he may not be worshipped according to the imaginations and devices of men, or the suggestions of Satan, under any visible representations or any other way not prescribed in the Holy Scripture."[4]

If this is the first time you've come across this way of understanding, it might seem horribly restrictive. Shouldn't we be free to worship any way we want that seems fitting? Doesn't the regulative principle box us in?

In fact, I'd suggest the exact opposite: rightly understood, this Reformed approach to worship is tremendously freeing. Let me suggest three "fears" it sets us free from. Or, to put the case more positively, we'll think of them as three blessings!

The Blessing of Pleasing God

When we thought about the purpose of worship, we focused on two truths about God. The first was that he is worthy of all praise: he is a God who deserves everything. When we come into his presence, then, how can we be sure we're worshipping him in a way that pleases him?

Not long after I got married, a well-meaning relative of my wife's, who knew Georgina had married "some sort of priest," sent us a belated wedding gift. As I unwrapped it, a wooden frame fell out, holding a gold-gilded icon of someone. I'm still not entirely sure who it is—the inscription is in Russian—presumably either Jesus or a saint. It was well intentioned but totally confused: Presbyterian pastors are really not into Russian Orthodox iconography! But I sympathize with the woman who bought it: she'd never met me and so had no real idea what I liked. Along similar lines, and with rather more guilt, I so misjudged the three Christmas presents I bought my wife for our first Christmas that every single one went back to the shop. Even the one she couldn't get a refund for ...

We want our worship to be a pleasing offering to God. We don't want to be guessing what he likes—what will delight him and what will displease him. This is why Reformed worship is so freeing. We do what God tells us to do—and therefore what pleases him. We're freed from the fear that we're somehow mis-stepping. And, more significantly still, we can be humbly confident that in coming only in the name of Christ, and worshipping in the manner he teaches, we are delighting our merciful heavenly Father.

The Blessing of Meeting God

As we've seen, worship is all about meeting with God. But where is he to be found? Where do we encounter his grace? Christians can get themselves in a total panic about how to meet God. What can we do to draw him near? How can we create an atmosphere where we'll feel his presence? How do we foster an environment that allows a true encounter? And how would we know if it worked?

Again, this is where a Reformed approach to worship is so freeing. It frees us from the search for God and instead focuses our attention on his coming to us in the ways and places he has laid out. Primary among these in the new covenant is the Word. As we saw with Jesus's conversation with the woman at the well, God no longer dwells in a temple in Jerusalem. There is no sacred place on earth where we must journey in order to meet him. Instead, he comes to us through what are often called the *means of grace.* According to the Westminster Shorter Catechism, "the outward and ordinary means whereby Christ communicates to us the benefits of redemption are his ordinances, especially the Word, sacraments and prayer; all which are made effectual to the elect for salvation."[5]

We know we want to meet God. We know he comes to us in Christ the Savior. But when I wake up on Sunday morning, Christ is in heaven and I am on earth. So how can I find him? The beautifully simple answer is that he has told me where he will meet his people to bless them: through these God-ordained means, particularly the Bible and the sacraments (baptism and the Lord's Supper). When we center our worship around these elements, we can be humbly confident of meeting the Lord, whatever we *feel* during the service.

We'd love to burst with joy each Lord's Day. We'd love to be stirred in the depths of our hearts with a renewed desire for God and a renewed desire to serve him. For a thousand reasons, sometimes the emotional experience of a Sunday service falls short of feeling like we've been caught up to the third heaven. But does that mean God hasn't met with us? No. We can be confident that as we humbly seek his blessing through the means he provides, he will be doing us good, whether we're weeping or in raptures of joy.

That is why Reformed worship services revolve solely around the elements God has provided. Is it *possible* God might work outside these "ordinary means of grace"? Of course! But our call is not to go to where it's *possible* God might meet us. It's possible he might speak through a donkey—he has done so before (see Num. 22:30)! But does that mean it's sensible to head to the local animal sanctuary on Sunday morning? Of course not! Might God write on a wall if we sit in silence? Might he send the angel Gabriel to visit? I suppose it's just about possible to imagine, at a stretch—he's done both before—though there's plenty in the New Testament that reminds us the Bible is now complete, and sufficient, containing everything we need to know for now (see 2 Tim. 3:16; Heb. 1:1–2). But even if you granted it was possible, that's still to miss the point.

Last Tuesday I arrived back from a two-week trip to the United States. My wife said she'd meet me at 3 p.m. at Leeds station. After two weeks away, I was understandably keen to see her. So where did I go? It's conceivable she *could* have been in the coffee shop at 1 p.m. or the grocery store at 2 p.m. But I acted on the basis of her promise and headed to the station at 3 p.m. to meet her. So too with God—yes, he can work outside the ordinary means should he so wish. But it's so freeing to know I don't need to desperately search around trying to find him. He will be where he said he'll be: meeting his people through his appointed means of grace.

The Blessing of Christ's Leading

So Reformed worship is meant to free us from displeasing God and from fearing doing so. It's meant to free us from the fear that we're not going to meet with Christ or that we need to desperately search for ever new ways of encountering him. But it also frees you from something else—me. Or at least people like me. Week by week I plan the worship service at Christ Church Central, Leeds. On Sunday the church assembles, and we follow through the various elements as I've planned them. After all, I'm the minister, so isn't it my call what we do when we worship?

Thankfully—not really. Of course there are choices to be made, and someone has to make them. In Reformed churches, that is most likely going to be one of the elders, those who are entrusted with oversight of the church under Christ. Elders have been appointed to teach, preach, lead, and minister in his name in accordance with his Word.

Look again, though, at the last two phrases of the last two sentences. Elders minister *under Christ* and *in accordance with his Word*. The authority of the elders is not absolute—not by any means. There are all sorts of limits put on the authority of church leaders in the New Testament, most of which would take us too far from the purposes of this book to explore. Abuse of power can be a terrible curse on the church. And yet at the same time elders are given real authority. Churches are told to "obey your leaders and submit to them" (Heb. 13:17). When it comes to the worship service, just what does that authority look like?

That authority is not the authority to innovate. Elders are not free to make God's people worship in ways other than the ones he has laid out in the Bible. Even if those things are not sinful in and of themselves, if they're not part of God's plan for corporate worship, we have no right to bind the consciences of people in the church by asking them to do things God hasn't required. Here's article 32 of the Belgic Confession, again picking up the theme of the freedom of Reformed worship: "We reject all human inventions, and all laws which man would introduce into the worship of God, thereby to bind and compel the conscience in any manner whatever."

Is it sinful to paint a picture of a beautiful sunset? To do a puppet show for children? To eat donuts and chat about football? Not at all! All these things could be perfectly valid uses of Christians' time as they live for God in all life. But should elders bring these activities into the church service, thereby forcing everyone to join in? No, that is beyond our authority. Christ has not commanded these things as part of worship, so we have no right to command people to perform them on our own authority. Instead, elders make secondary-level decisions, which essentially boil down to the manner in which we do the things Christ has told us to do. We know he wants the Word preached. But what passage should be preached this Sunday? For how long? In what language? These are decisions church leaders are authorized to make and indeed *must* make. So too with music. Should we sing? Yes! But which songs? How many? When during the service? The "what" of worship is God's prerogative alone. The "how" he gives us freedom to decide.

We'll return to this idea later as we think about what have traditionally been known as the *elements* and *circumstances* of worship. But again, it's freeing! The people of Christ Church Central, Leeds, are free from any crazy ideas that may pop into my head, free from being effectively forced to do things that are against their conscience—free indeed from anyone's ultimate authority but Christ's. This is, incidentally, a great freedom for ministers too. We are freed from the need to be endlessly creative and inventive! We don't need to discover new ways to engage or entertain God's people. Rather, we can build our services on the solid ground of God's Word and look to him to bless his appointed means.

Conclusion

Worship, the central meeting of God and his people, is initiated by God and governed by his Word. We, his sheep, are freed from all sorts of fears and anxieties as we walk the paths he lays out for us, drink at the quiet waters he prepares for us, and find rest in the green pastures he spreads before us. And all the time we are led by the Good Shepherd he sent to gather us. Just what form those pools and pastures take in this new covenant era is the next question to which we should turn our attention.

Questions for Further Reflection

1. What is the key principle of Reformed worship? How would you defend it from Scripture?
2. What are some of the blessings of this approach?
3. How might you answer the criticism that the regulative principle is boring and restrictive?

4

THE POWER AND PILLARS
OF WORSHIP

Given that worship is the right response to meeting God, it's no surprise that when the disciples met the risen Jesus at the end of Matthew's Gospel, "they worshiped him" (Matt. 28:17). What else would you do? Similarly the magi, the wise men, who had traveled from the East to Mary and Joseph's house, "fell down and worshiped him," small child though Jesus was (Matt. 2:11). Here are true worship experiences: meeting God in Christ and falling down in praise.

An Absent Christ?

But of course Christ has now returned to heaven. How can we meet him in light of this departure? The book of Acts answers this question. Jesus is in one sense truly absent—he ascended in front of the watching disciples and disappeared from sight. Whatever New Testament worship looks like, it's about faith, not sight.

But absence to the eye is not total absence. Jesus continues to be a prophet, priest, and king to his church (see Acts 26:23; Heb. 5:6; Rev. 1:5). Luke, who wrote Acts, hints at this in the very first verses:

> In the first book, O Theophilus, I have dealt with all that Jesus began to do and teach, until the day when he was taken up, after he had given commands through the Holy Spirit to the apostles whom he had chosen. (Acts 1:1–2)

Luke's first book is the gospel that bears his name. That book was about what Jesus *began* to do and teach. The strong implication is that Acts, which is essentially Luke's Gospel Part 2, is what Jesus *continued* to do and teach. That's significant. It would be easy to think that Jesus tapped out at the ascension and retired to heaven to put his feet up, perhaps leaving the rest of the work to the Holy Spirit. But that's not at all the case. Jesus remains the one Mediator between God and man, the one "place" we can meet God in safety.

How does this work now that he's physically left earth? There's a clue in the verses above. In the period after his resurrection but before the ascension, Jesus gave commands to the apostles "through the Holy Spirit" (Acts 1:2). The risen Christ continues his ministry through the Holy Spirit and via the apostles.

This is what Pentecost is all about. After Jesus returned to heaven, the Holy Spirit was poured out on the church—poured out by God (see Acts 2:17) and also by Jesus, who has received the Spirit from his Father (see Acts 2:33). After Pentecost, Jesus continues to come to his people, but from then on he works through the Holy Spirit. The Spirit is therefore vital to new covenant worship.

A Spiritual House

Pentecost is in some senses a reversal of the disaster at the Tower of Babel. Back in Genesis 11:1–9, God scattered a proud and arrogant people who sought to reach the heavens by their own endeavor. As part of his judgment, the languages of the world were confused and all the people were scattered. At Pentecost, the Holy Spirit was poured on the believers, who were supernaturally enabled to speak in all sorts of languages so that the gospel they proclaimed could be understood. The Holy Spirit had begun the work of gathering the scattered, of reuniting a new humanity in Christ who would approach God not with the works of their own hands, tower or otherwise, but in the name of Christ. He was forming a new temple.

Although each individual believer is described as a "temple of the Holy Spirit" (1 Cor. 6:19), the church images in the New Testament are primarily corporate. We are the "body of Christ" (1 Cor. 12:27). We are the "household of God" (Eph. 2:19). We, the church, are the temple of the Holy Spirit (see 1 Cor. 3:16–17). Paul's conclusion is striking:

> So then you are no longer strangers and aliens, but you are fellow citizens with the saints and members of the household of God, built on the foundation of the apostles and prophets, Christ Jesus himself being the cornerstone, in whom the whole structure, being joined together, grows into a holy temple in the Lord. In him you also are being built together into a dwelling place for God by the Spirit. (Eph. 2:19–22)

The Holy Spirit is building us together to be a dwelling place for God. It's no surprise that the New Testament word for church is *ecclesia*, which refers to an assembly. When the Jews translated the Old Testament into Greek before the coming of Jesus, they used this same word to describe the "day of assembly" we saw in a previous chapter. Indeed, it's the same word Stephen used to describe Israel as a "congregation in the wilderness"—we might just as well translate it as a *church* in the wilderness (Acts 7:38). Elsewhere, James calls the local church a "synagogue"—picking up the Jewish name for the local gatherings of Jews dispersed around the world (James 2:2; the ESV translates this as "assembly"). And Paul speaks of the church in Corinth assembling—the verb is literally to "synagogue"—when they gather to meet.[1]

We have a tendency to individualize the Christian life. What *really* matters, we think, is *my* personal prayer time, *my* personal Bible reading, *my* personal relationship with Jesus. Church is perhaps a useful "top up" to refuel us for our walk during the rest of the week. Or perhaps it's the place we go primarily to encourage one another to keep going in the Christian life. There are, of course, elements of truth here. Church should be an encouragement. It's good to pray on your own! But the New Testament's emphasis is on the church gathered.

The Spirit does his work by gathering and assembling God's people. The main tools Christ uses to bless his people are necessarily corporate. Think of preaching or partaking in the Lord's Supper. These aren't possible to do at home alone! In fact, for most of the history of God's work in the world, most of God's people couldn't read the Bible alone for the simple reasons that they didn't own the Scriptures and wouldn't be able to read them even if they did!

None of this is in any way to denigrate personal discipleship. Rather, it's to put gathered, corporate worship back where it belongs: at the center of our Christian lives. Corporate worship is the sun around which personal and family devotions rotate. Likewise, it's revolutionary to realize the main theater of the Spirit's work is in the gathered church at worship. We can approach the Sunday service with great expectation, knowing we're entering the realm of his gracious activity.

Men at Work

As the church gathers on Sunday, the spiritual house assembles. People young and old take their seats and then . . . what? If Christ comes to us by the Spirit, does he call us to sit and wait until the Spirit "shows up" and does something? At times in the history of the church, groups have done more or less just that. They have sat in silence, hoping the Spirit would visit or inspire someone to speak. This approach, though, is far from the one laid out by Jesus himself.

Think back to Christ's final instructions to the disciples before he returned to heaven. This passage is so famous that it's been given a name: the Great Commission. So what exactly did he commission the disciples to do? Head home, gather next Sunday, and see what happens? No.

> And Jesus came and said to them, "All authority in heaven and on earth has been given to me. Go therefore and make disciples of all nations, baptizing them in the name of the Father and of the Son and of the Holy Spirit, teaching them to observe all that I have commanded you. And behold, I am with you always, to the end of the age." (Matt. 28:18–20)

Much in this short passage is significant for us. First of all, notice that Christ, while retaining all authority in himself, sent the disciples out to work. The power is still his—his promise was "I will build my church" (Matt. 16:18), not "You will go and build it for me." But Jesus would do the building through the apostles' ministry. In particular, they were to teach and baptize. These represent the two "tools" of Christian ministry: the Word and sacraments. We'll look in more detail at both in a minute, but for now we need to see that they were given to the church to be stewarded by Christ's appointed leaders.

Paul develops this theme in his letter to the Ephesians. Spot again the link between "church officers," the people called to ministry, and the Word they are to minister. It would be worth taking a moment to read Ephesians 4:1–16 to see these verses in context. Christ has ascended, but as he did so he showered gifts on the church (see Eph. 4:4–8). We might expect Paul to list some classic gifts: serving, teaching, prophesying, and so on. But he went in a different direction:

> And he gave the apostles, the prophets, the evangelists, the shepherds and teachers, to equip the saints for the work of ministry, for building up the body of Christ, until we all attain to the unity of the faith and of the knowledge of the Son of God, to mature manhood, to the measure of the stature of the fullness of Christ. (Eph. 4:11–13)

The spiritual gifts are . . . people. Specifically, they're church officers: men appointed to the work of ministry.

The Reformed understanding is that *apostles* and *prophets* were commissioned by Christ to speak his very Word, which is why Paul said that the church is "built on the foundation of the apostles and prophets" (Eph. 2:20). These are the men who wrote the Scriptures. No one nowadays serves in either of these roles.[2] For one thing, to be an apostle, you had to have been with Jesus during his earthly ministry (see Acts 1:21–22)! There's some debate as to what Paul means by an *evangelist*. But all are agreed that the offices of *shepherds* and *teachers* continue in our day. Some read this as one role: shepherds who are teachers. Others see a distinction. But Presbyterian churches, directed by the New Testament, are always overseen by elders.[3]

However you parse out the relationship between what have traditionally been called "teaching elders" (or pastors or ministers) and "ruling elders"—a subject that would take us too far away from our current focus—the basic point is clear: Christ teaches and leads his church through these appointed men. Church officers are not a human invention or a committee elected for convenience's sake. Paul can say to the group of elders in Ephesus that it was the Holy Spirit who appointed them (see Acts 20:28)! Elders are Christ's servants through whom he ministers to his people.

To be clear, the power and the authority mentioned by Jesus in his Great Commission are not found in the elders themselves. These men are servants of the Word, called, among other things, to faithfully teach and oversee the sacraments of baptism and the Lord's Supper. Yet the fact that they are "men like us" shouldn't undermine the fact that they are the people Christ uses to build up his church. Just look at what Ephesians 4:13 tells us Christ does through these faithful preachers: he gives knowledge, maturity, and fullness to the church.

The ministry of the Word is utterly central to any worship service. And that ministry has been entrusted to the church's elders. This is why if you attend a church in the Reformed tradition it's likely that at the very least the preaching, and most likely the leading and praying, are conducted by an elder. Elders are not priests, allowed closer to God than everyone else, go-betweens who mediate your relationship with Christ. There is only one Great High Priest, and one Mediator, Christ. But ministers are one of the chief tools Jesus uses to bless and strengthen his church. To them has been entrusted this work of ministry, so pray for them to serve faithfully in their Master's house.

The Word at Work

As we've spoken about pastors and teachers, I hope it's become clear that their duty is to preach and teach the Word of God, the Bible. The Word is the chief means of grace, the ordinary way that Christ gives life to his people. Peter reminds the believers he writes to that they "have been born again, not of perishable seed but of imperishable, through the living and enduring word of God" (1 Peter 1:23). Time and again in the Gospels, we see Jesus speaking an ordinary-sounding word with supernatural results. Devils are driven out, the blind see, and with a word—"Lazarus, come out!"—a dead man is raised. A pastor who doesn't preach God's Word has no authority whatsoever and is of no use to the church.

Does this mean that it is the Bible, not the Holy Spirit, that contains the real power? No. If it were the case that simply hearing the Bible brought spiritual life, all we'd need to do to evangelize the world is blast John 3:16 on a loudspeaker in each city, town, and village. All we'd need to do to sanctify the church would be to make sure each Christian heard each word of Scripture and boom, job done. But we know that's not the case: Jesus warned as much in the parable of the sower in Matthew 13:1–23.

So what do we do with the fact that life and power are attributed to both the Word and the Holy Spirit? The Reformed answer to this question is to see that the Spirit uses the Word to achieve his purposes. The Spirit comes with the Word to bring life, holiness, encouragement, rebuke, comfort, challenge. Of course, he can choose to work without the Word. But we're not interested in what God the Spirit *might* do—that is his prerogative. Calvin put it like this: "For, although God's power is not bound to outward means, he has nonetheless bound us to this ordinary manner of teaching."[4]

What we want to know is where we should go when we know we're in desperate need of Christ's life-giving Spirit. The answer is to the Word. But we're not to approach God's Word, read and preached, relying on our own intellectual resources. Sermons are not lectures; Bible readings are not English comprehension exercises. The English theologian and pastor John Owen, who among other things wrote a seven-volume commentary on the book of Hebrews, said that without the Holy Spirit we may as well burn our Bibles.[5] Similarly, when Dutch theologian Herman Bavinck was reflecting on the Reformed tradition, he wrote that "the Reformers jointly maintained that the Word alone is insufficient to bring people to faith and repentance."[6] The power is in Christ's Spirit. It is in his sovereign gift to make the reading and preaching of God's Word effectual.

There are therefore two errors we may fall into when we seek to meet Christ by his Spirit. The first is to ignore the "ordinary means," especially the Word, and seek some other channel of blessing, some other way to "engage the Spirit." The second—perhaps more of a danger in Reformed, Bible-preaching churches—is to treat the Bible as if it is a document we master. At times—and with a horrible irony—we can almost mirror the Roman Catholic approach to sacraments. Just as Roman Catholicism teaches that the sacraments work almost automatically, by virtue of administering them—baptism bestows grace by its very act—so Bible-loving Protestants can begin to act as if just being there for a sermon or listening to a Scripture reading necessarily brings blessing.

Instead we should approach the Word the same way Bartimaeus approached Jesus: "Son of David have mercy on me. . . . Let me recover my sight" (Mark 10:47–51). We rely entirely on his ministry to us through his Spirit.

Soaked in the Word

If the Word is the chief means of grace, how does that affect our worship services? It means, clearly, that we should want them to be saturated with Scripture. Dr. Ligon Duncan, a Presbyterian pastor and theologian, gives a neat summary. We are to "read the Bible, preach the Bible, pray the Bible, sing the Bible, and see the Bible."[7] We'll look at each of these elements later, but it helps to express the idea that having a Word-centered service doesn't mean just having a Bible reading and sermon. We want the Word to permeate our prayers, songs, calls to worship, assurances of pardon, and closing benedictions.

I used to live in Derbyshire, one of the most beautiful of all the English counties. One part of the county has a particularly extensive network of caves running under it. So extensive, in fact, that no one had ever mapped them out or knew quite where they ran. Because many were filled with water, someone came up with the bright idea of flushing purple dye through the tunnels to see where it came out. The answer was pretty much everywhere! Over the next few days, flowers in people's gardens changed color as they sucked up the dye, and ponds and village wells turned purple: the underground streams went everywhere. This is what we want for our services: we want them to be dyed through with the Word of God.

When Paul is trying to sort out the chaos in the Corinthian church worship services, it's striking that so many of the things going on are "Word" activities: prophecies, words of instruction, hymns, revelations, and so on. The Word comes to us in different forms—sung, read, preached, prayed—but it colors everything we do.

The Pillars of Worship

When we think about worship, there's a danger that we'll rush straight to a list of dos and don'ts, as if biblical worship boils down to a checklist. That's why we've spent some time trying to understand what goes on when we worship, how God—Father, Son, and Holy Spirit—is active in worship, and why we come to worship in the first place. With those things in place, we can turn our attention to the regulative principle and the specifics of a service.

Remember the basic idea behind the regulative principle is that we only do in worship what God commands. These things have come to be known as the *elements* of worship. They are, if you like, the building blocks of a service, the pillars that the service is structured on. Elements tell us what we're meant to do—not that you necessarily need every element each time. Different churches have different understandings, for example, of how often you should celebrate the Lord's Supper. Few churches are blessed to see baptisms each week. Ultimately, it is the Spirit-brought Word that is the "irreducible minimum" of a true meeting with God.

But what are these elements? The Westminster Confession gives a typical answer:

The reading of the Scriptures with godly fear; the sound preaching and conscionable hearing of the Word, in obedience unto God, with understanding, faith, and reverence; singing of psalms with grace in the heart; as, also, the due administration and worthy receiving of the sacraments instituted by Christ; are all parts of the ordinary religious worship of God: besides religious oaths, vows, solemn fastings, and thanksgivings upon several occasions; which are, in their several times and seasons, to be used in an holy and religious manner.[8]

If you look at this list, you'll see that it boils down to two basic categories. First are those "means of grace" that Christ uses to bless his people, principally the Word and sacraments. Then there are a host of activities that describe our right response to God coming to us in grace. So the preached Word is a means of grace. Our response is "conscionable" (diligent) hearing. The Lord's Supper is a means of grace. Our response is "worthy receiving." Likewise, we sing God's praise, pray to him, and, where appropriate, make vows such as baptismal promises. Many, including Calvin, add the giving of offerings and gifts as an acceptable element.

When the Westminster Confession was first written, the English parliament asked the gathered ministers and theologians to go back and add proof texts. This they did with some reluctance. (For reasons of space I've included these in the endnotes.[9]) The authors were scrupulous to find biblical warrant for each element. The description of the early church gathering shortly after Pentecost was particularly significant:

And they devoted themselves to the apostles' teaching and the fellowship, to the breaking of bread and the prayers. And awe came upon every soul, and many wonders and signs were being done through the apostles. And all who believed were together and had all things in common. And they were selling their possessions and belongings and distributing the proceeds to all, as any had need. (Acts 2:42–44)

In the next chapter we'll walk through some of these elements and see how they fit into a typical service. But, before we do so, there's one more term we need to grapple with if we're to understand Reformed worship.

Circumstances

A common critique of the regulative principle, especially from those who come across it for the first time, is that it's broken by its adherents every week. "Does the Bible tell you to use hymnbooks? Give me the Bible verse that says you should stand up to sing. Where does Scripture tell you it's OK to use a microphone and sound system?"

This challenge, however well meant, misses the key distinction between the *elements* and *circumstances* of worship. *Elements*, as we've seen, are the "what" of worship. *Circumstances* is the term that has come to be used of the "how" of worship. Preaching is an element. How long you preach for, how many verses you cover, whether you stand or sit to do so—these things are all circumstances.

Even the staunchest defender of the regulative principle admits—or rather happily acknowledges—that in these circumstances we have to be guided by common sense, wisdom, and the light of nature. It's probably not smart, for example, to attempt to sing through the entire book of Psalms during each Sunday morning service. But I can't give you a Bible verse that tells you that! Questions such as what time of day to meet, where to meet, whether to have hymns projected onto the wall or printed in a bulletin all touch on circumstantial issues.

Supernaturally Ordinary

Supernaturally ordinary is a phrase I love to use about our ministry in my church at Leeds. It captures, I hope, what we believe about worship. Anyone who comes along would find our services to be in one sense tremendously ordinary. There's nothing particularly jazzy about them, no surprises or inventiveness. We try our best to do everything well: the music, the physical setup, the preaching, the bulletin, and so on. We're not advocating laziness or sloppiness in approaching God! But we're an ordinary congregation of pretty ordinary people, led by pretty ordinary elders.

And yet the ordinariness shouldn't lead us to believe nothing supernatural is going on! The Holy Spirit by definition works supernaturally: he is not a "natural" being.

We may be tempted to think that *supernatural* equates to weird, unexpected, spectacular. If the Holy Spirit was *really* at work, we think, things would get pretty extraordinary. Again, while I'm not denying that God can do what he wants when he wants, I think this view is misguided. We can't pretend to *really* understand how the Holy Spirit works. We can see it's often through the Word. But how?

When Pastor Jeff gets up to preach, we might describe what happens in purely physical terms: Jeff's lungs push out air, shaped by his tongue and lips, that vibrates across the room and strikes Reuben's eardrum, which causes electro-magnetic signals to be sent to his brain. . . . I'm wildly out of my depth here, as you may be able to tell, but you get the idea. All so ordinary. And yet, in the mysterious working of the Spirit, as a result of that wobbling air, Reuben may be converted, or have his eyes opened further to the grace of God, or see the horror of his sin, or . . . We can't explain it. It looks so normal. Yet that is how God delights to work. After all, if we'd been watching God's greatest act in the history of the world, we'd have seen what to all intents and purposes looked like another run-of-the-mill thirtysome-thing Jewish carpenter being executed in ignominy. And yet in that moment God supernaturally changed everything!

He Knows Not How

I hope this is a real encouragement as you approach worship this coming Sunday. We don't need to chase the thrill, the spiritual high, the dramatic encounter. It's not that emotion is bad—far from it! Just that having emotional experiences and meeting God in his grace are not the same thing. The Spirit works in secret, and the Word does its work buried deep in the hearts and minds of God's people.

Remember the parable of the seed: "The kingdom of God is as if a man should scatter seed on the ground. He sleeps and rises night and day, and the seed sprouts and grows; he knows not how" (Mark 4:26–27). The seed, the Word of God, is sown. Then the sower goes to sleep! When it grows, "he knows not how." The preacher's job is to preach faithfully, and the congregation's is to put themselves under the preached Word. After that, the results lie in the hands of Christ and his Spirit.

One of my friends once wrote about a new ministry he was starting: "Clueless Church." The tagline was "He knows not how." It was entirely tongue-in-cheek, but the point is still a good one. None of us really knows what the Holy Spirit is doing. That doesn't mean we revert to mysticism, sitting around hoping something will happen. No, we attend to the means of grace. But we do so with patience. Apparently the Church of England minister Charles Bridges used to tell his trainee preachers, "The Word you sow may lie underground until you do!" Wise words to fuel a supernaturally ordinary ministry.

Questions for Further Reflection

1. What is the role of the Holy Spirit in worship?
2. What role do pastors and elders play in worship? Having read this chapter, do you think you tend to have too high or too low a view of them? Why?
3. What are the means of grace? What is their significance?
4. What two mistakes might we make in regards to the means of grace? Which do you feel is more likely in your church setting? How might you guard against it?
5. What is the difference between the elements and the circumstances of worship?

THE PATTERN OF WORSHIP

One of the aspects of Reformed worship services that commonly surprises people is their structured, patterned nature. If we've come from a charismatic or Pentecostal church background, we may be used to thinking that "structured" and "spiritual" are more or less opposites—that spontaneity is the sign of the Holy Spirit at work. To plan in advance is to take the life out of our gatherings, to rely on human thinking rather than the dynamic movement of the Spirit.

Yet through most of the history of the church, great care has been put into the order of the service. Congregations haven't gathered to "see where the Spirit leads." Rather, pastors charged with the leading of worship have prayerfully sought the Spirit's leading in advance of Sunday, guided as ever by the Spirit's chief tool, the Word of God.

Structures and Stories

"Structures tell stories."[1] So begins Bryan Chapell in his tremendously helpful introduction to Christ-centered worship. It's true of physical structures: a cinema, football stadium, coffee shop, or clothes store is designed to shape our behavior in specific ways. These structures subtly convey messages to those who enter—cheer, buy, sit, watch—just by their shape and design. What's true of physical buildings is also true of worship services.

Chapell shows that almost every church tradition has carefully thought through the order to its worship service—and indeed many of those orders end up being remarkably similar. Traditionally, this pattern is known as the *liturgy*. I'm not for a minute going to suggest that there is one set liturgy that every church ought to follow. But that doesn't mean there's no wisdom at all to be found in reflecting on what a healthy new covenant liturgy might look like. Indeed, God has woven some patterns of worship into the created order.

Structure and Sabbath

In the beginning, God made the heaven and earth. That would be all the information we'd need to understand where we and our universe came from. Yet we get more detail: we learn that God created all things over a period of six days, but then came a seventh day:

> And on the seventh day God finished his work that he had done, and he rested on the seventh day from all his work that he had done. So God blessed the seventh day

and made it holy, because on it God rested from all his work that he had done in creation. (Gen. 2:2–3)

This seventh day was set aside from the others when it was declared holy. In the Old Testament system of thought, to be holy was to be particularly set aside for God's use. Thus you might have lots of candlesticks, but a holy candlestick was separated for use in the tabernacle, God's house. There were many nations, but Israel, God's special people, was a holy nation. All peoples—and for that matter all candlesticks—belong to him, but some were particularly "sanctified," made holy, for his use. So too the seventh day. Of course, all days are God's. But the seventh was set aside as a day *for* him. It was a day of rest: *Sabbath* is a word derived from the Hebrew verb meaning "to cease." And it was a day of worship.

This becomes all the clearer as the story continues. In the fourth commandment, God's people are told to observe the Sabbath day and keep it holy by resting from their work. Again, there's a combination of rest and worship: the day is a "Sabbath *to the* Lord" (Deut. 5:14). In other words, God isn't commanding us to sleep all Sabbath. The day is the one separated out from the others for us to gather to worship the Lord. In case anyone be in any doubt, God makes the connection unmissable in Leviticus: "Six days shall work be done, but on the seventh day is a Sabbath of solemn rest, a holy convocation" (Lev. 23:3).

At the start of a chapter on various worship feasts and festivals, the regular feast day of worship heads the list. That's why Luke tells us it was Jesus's custom to be in the synagogue each Sabbath, gathered with the Lord's people (see Luke 4:16). As has hopefully become clear throughout this book, it is God who sets the agenda when it comes to his worship. He controls his people's calendars. And each week he has written in a day for us to cease work and gather to worship.

Of course, in the new covenant there is a change. But the change is to which day we gather rather than to the very idea of God having an appointed day. Rather than gathering on the seventh day (Saturday, as we'd call it), we now gather on the first day of the week, Sunday. This is, of course, the day of resurrection, the day Jesus arose from the tomb to meet with his people. If you read about Jesus's several appearances following the resurrection, you'll see that they're repeatedly on Sundays (see John 20:1, 19, 26).[2] Similarly, when we get almost offhand comments about when the New Testament church gathered, it's on the first day of the week (see Acts 20:7; 1 Cor. 16:2). This wouldn't have been the convenient day to meet in Jewish culture: everyone else was resting and worshipping on Saturday. So why make things awkward and meet on Sunday? Only because it was the Lord's appointed day, so the church met at his command.

In fact, very few things are explicitly said to belong to the Lord in the New Testament. Discounting angels and body parts (the Lord's feet and so on), it's pretty much just the Lord's Supper, cup, and table (see 1 Cor. 10:21; 11:20) and the Lord's Day (see Rev. 1:10). Do all suppers belong to the Lord? In a sense, of course, yes. But that doesn't mean there isn't a special Supper, set aside for his worship. Do all days belong to him? Again, yes, but there remains one day he has appointed to meet with his people through the resurrected Christ.[3]

This is why Reformed churches meet to worship on Sunday. The elders haven't sat down to work out what day is most convenient or when most people can get there. Still less have they researched which time of the week you're most likely to get non-Christians to visit. Rather, they have chosen a time on Sunday, the first day of the week. In doing so, they are following God's pattern for worship.

The move to the first day of the week is meant, among other things, to remind us that we are no longer looking forward in hope to a Savior to come. Rather, he has already appeared, done everything necessary to redeem his people, and brought them to rest. As we celebrate that rescue, we begin the week from a position of fullness. Everything has been done.

The Puritans uses to call Sunday the "market day of the soul." Back before supermarkets and convenience stores, villagers would stock up once a week on the day the market came to town. You'd fill your basket with everything you needed for the week ahead and then live off those supplies until the next market day arrived. Similarly, we head to church to have our souls fed and filled with the good things Christ has stored up for us. Those resources fuel us for the week to come. Whatever the state of our personal discipleship, "quiet times," and so on, we have a great market day fixed firmly in the diary, where we know we'll find good food for the soul, brought to us by a good Master who invites us to buy without money or price.

Structured Services in the Old Testament

So God has given us a structure to the week. But what about the worship itself? Does God have anything to say about the pattern of our worship when we draw near? In the days of the old covenant, the answer was certainly yes. We've already mentioned the feasts and festivals that structured the Israelite year. Each of these had detailed instructions that guided priest and worshipper alike through the celebration.

Significant for our purposes are the offerings and sacrifices of Leviticus. These were the lifeblood of old covenant worship. Reading Leviticus, perhaps during a "Bible in a year" plan, can be confusing. There seem to be endless rules and regulations that are hard to follow, especially at several thousand years remove. But in essence the central offerings were fairly simple and clear in their message. There are five main offerings: the burnt offering, grain offering, peace offering, sin offering, and guilt offering. Although they're presented in this order in Leviticus 1–5, whenever we read of anyone actually making a sacrifice, the order is different—and always the same. It's an order that, once you get hold of it, makes perfect sense.[4]

The first offering is always the sin or guilt offering. These are the "atoning" offerings, made in response to specific sins and breaches of God's law. In each an animal is sacrificed and dies in place of the sinner. After this comes the burnt offering or, in a more literal translation, the "ascension" offering. This time, the focus is on transformation. The whole animal is consumed by fire on the altar (hence the ESV calling it a "burnt" offering, even though the word translated "burnt" literally means "going up"). The emphasis is on the sacrificed animal being transformed into smoke and "going up" symbolically from the bronze altar out in the tabernacle courtyard to the gold altar in the Holy Place. It's as if the worshipper, represented by the animal, has had his sin atoned for and is cleansed and transformed, made fit to enter God's house proper.

With this offering (never on its own) comes the grain offering. This time no animal dies: sacrifice and atonement are over. The grain offering is a gift to God: Who would want to come before the Lord emptyhanded? Interestingly, the offering is to be mixed with incense and oil. Bread, incense, and oil: the three things you'd find in the Holy Place, the tabernacle proper, in the form of the oil-burning lampstand, the bread of the presence, and the altar of incense. This is a gift fit for the King!

Finally comes the peace offering. Again an animal dies, but this time there is no talk of atonement or forgiveness. That is done and dusted at this stage of worship. Instead, this is an offering that, uniquely, the offerer shares in. Some of the animal is consumed on the altar, a food offering for God. But some is eaten by the Israelite. The whole worship experience ends in fellowship. The meal doesn't make peace but proclaims and celebrates a peace that has been achieved by the atoning sacrifices.[5]

Can you see the gospel pattern? Atonement, transformation, fellowship. Christ dies for us, we are transformed by the Spirit, and one day we will feast with him in heaven. Old Testament structured worship prophesied the great work of redemption.

We could look at other Old Testament passages that have a similar gospel shape. As Isaiah comes before the presence of the Lord, we see him being overcome by the holiness of God (Isa. 6:1–4), confessing his sin (v. 5), being assured of atonement and pardon (vv. 6–7), responding in service (v. 8), and receiving the Word of God to instruct him and send him out to God's people (v. 9). Or there's the basic structure of God's meeting with his people at Mount Sinai. There are various cycles, but focusing on Exodus 24 we see God's call (vv. 1–2), an atoning sacrifice (vv. 5–6), consecration through the Word (v. 7), and then a meal with God (vv. 9–11).[6] Old Testament worship is structured to tell the story of the gospel.

Structured Services in the New Testament

But what about when we come to the New Testament and indeed our own day? We've already said there's no one pattern that's made explicitly binding in the New Testament. It would be an overstatement to say that all Reformed churches have at all times followed a particular pattern of worship. And yet there has been what you might call a "majority position." The church services designed by the likes of Martin Luther, John Calvin, Thomas Cranmer, John Knox, the Westminster Assembly, and countless Reformed churches down through the intervening centuries have borne remarkable similarities to one another. This is no coincidence. Each has sought to be informed and shaped by the patterns of Old Testament worship, the gospel story itself, and the historical wisdom of the church.

So, while once again reaffirming that this isn't binding in the same way as some of the other worship-related topics we've discussed, we'll walk through a "typical" Reformed liturgy and try to understand the story it is telling. That story is the story of the gospel. In fact, many Presbyterians understand their services to be times of "covenant renewal." It's not that between Sundays we've fallen out of covenant relationship with God and the covenant needs remaking. These are services of *renewal*, not restarting or remaking. Just as you and your spouse might sit down together, confess sin to each other, forgive each other, embrace, kiss, and talk about how your marriage covenant will look from now on, so God meets with us and we walk through a similar pattern. Except in our case forgiveness is only needed by one party! The married couple is not remarrying. Rather they are, as it were, renewing the existing and binding marriage covenant. So too as we gather to worship each Sunday. It is because we are part of the glorious, gracious, eternal new covenant that we dare draw near to have that covenant-shaped relationship renewed and strengthened.

Because of this covenant shape, worship services are like a dialogue. God speaks, and we respond appropriately. He is always the one ministering, really doing the work. We are beggars, receiving with empty hands. So as we move through a typical Reformed order of service, spot the giving and receiving pattern as the Lord speaks and his people reply. Again, not all Reformed services will be structured in this way: it is not commanded by God's Word. But many do, so it's worth understanding why!

Gospel-Shaped Worship

God Speaks: Call to Worship

Worship begins with God's Word. It is God who initiates his relationship with us and God who calls us to meet with him again in worship. Straightaway we are being reminded that we are not the center of the universe. Rather, we exist for the glory of another and live to serve at his command. Typically this call might come from a psalm:

Make a joyful noise to the LORD, all the earth!
  Serve the LORD with gladness!
  Come into his presence with singing! (Ps. 100:1–2)

This is the day that the LORD has made;
  let us rejoice and be glad in it. (Ps. 118:24)

Right from the outset we are reminded of the incredibly good news that God in Christ *wants* to meet with his people. We are hearing the Good Shepherd once again call his sheep to him, however far they've wandered that week and however filthy they've become in the mires and ditches of sin.

God's People Respond: Prayer of Invocation and Adoration

Having been called to appear before him, the church responds by asking for God's help to worship. This is known as a *prayer of invocation*, a calling on God to bless his people. Alongside this, many churches pray in praise to God, celebrating his grace, glory, and goodness. This could be said or sung. Often in Reformed churches opening hymns focus on God's character.

God Speaks: Reading of the Law, Invitation to Confession of Sin

How did Isaiah respond to meeting God? By falling down and confessing his sin. After God's initial call, the second "act" of the worship story begins with God's reminding us of how we ought to live. Perhaps the Ten Commandments are read, or Jesus's summary of the law known as the Great Commandment. Many churches combine this with an invitation to confess sin. This may be a promise of cleansing for all who come in Christ's name. It may be a reminder of the grace and mercy of the Lord.

I like to think of this invitation as a way of getting Adam out of the bush. When Adam became aware of his sin, he ran to hide in the hedge. It was a futile plan but in one sense understandable. For a sinner to come face-to-face with God is terrifying. There is, of course, nowhere to hide. But we're fools, and instead of fleeing to God for mercy, we run away. The law alone won't get us out of the bush: it reminds us of the reason we ought to be in there in the first place! This itself is a good thing. It humbles us and reminds us of our need for grace. But it's the gospel that gets us out of hiding and reminds us that it is a safe thing—indeed, the only safe thing—to come to God in confession.

> If we say we have no sin, we deceive ourselves, and the truth is not in us. If we confess our sins, he is faithful and just to forgive us our sins and to cleanse us from all unrighteousness. (1 John 1:8–9)

> For you, O Lord, are good and forgiving,
>   abounding in steadfast love to all who call upon you.
>   (Ps. 86:5)

God's People Respond: Corporate Confession of Sin

Again God's people come before him in prayer, this time in confession of sin. Perhaps one of the penitential psalms is used, such as Psalm 51 or 130. Perhaps the congregation uses a prayer from a historic liturgy. Maybe the pastor has crafted a prayer that fits with the wider structure of the service.

God Speaks: Assurance of Pardon

This is one of my favorite moments of the service. On the authority of God's Word, the pastor reminds and reassures the congregation that they are forgiven. Perhaps he focuses on the character of God. Perhaps he reaches for a "gospel promise." Perhaps he uses a story of an encounter with Jesus. Whatever the details, it's crucial to remember the pastor is speaking on behalf of the Lord who has appointed him. This is good news that comes not just from the pulpit but from the throne room of heaven.

We all need the gospel to be preached to us again and again and again. It is a word that comes from outside us, not something that we instinctively feel from within. Through the assurance of pardon, the word of comfort, Christ comes again to his people to remind them that they are at peace with their God.

> There is therefore now no condemnation for those who are in Christ Jesus. (Rom. 8:1)

The saying is trustworthy and deserving of full acceptance, that Christ Jesus came into the world to save sinners, of whom I am the foremost. (1 Tim. 1:15)

God's People Respond: Prayers of Intercession

At this point, reaffirmed in our status as beloved children of God, we boldly approach the throne of grace with all our prayers and petitions. Writing to Timothy, Paul spoke of various "types" of prayer: "I urge that supplications, prayers, intercessions, and thanksgivings be made for all people" (1 Tim. 2:1). Paul isn't wasting words. These are all prayers, but they are prayers that concern different things. His list emphasizes that our services should have a rich diet of prayer.

"Intercessions" are when we bring the needs of God's people and God's world before the King on God's throne. Often known as "the long prayer" or "the pastoral prayer," this is the prayer in which the pastor leads the congregation in bringing the suffering, sick, and sin-burdened to God. Although the pastor may be the one speaking, the whole congregation is praying. They are like the friends who brought the paralyzed man to Jesus: he couldn't get there himself, so they carried him.

There's some debate as to whether prayer should be counted as a means of grace. Reformed theologian Herman Bavinck writes, "Strictly speaking, the Word and the sacraments alone can be viewed as means of grace."[7] If the means involve the Spirit's ministry to us, then perhaps it's better to understand prayer as the chief way we *receive* this grace. Prayer, including psalms and hymns, is an element of worship, but it sits on the "church response" side of the dialogue.

God Speaks: The Reading and Preaching of the Word

Unsurprisingly, the reading of the Bible is central to the Reformed worship service. Indeed, without the Word, worship wouldn't be able to take place at all, given that it's through the Word that Christ meets with his church. Churches differ on how many readings they have, although many take one from the Old Testament and one from the New. Each pastor is picking up the mantle Paul laid on Timothy: "Devote yourself to the public reading of Scripture" (1 Tim. 4:13).

Likewise, Paul exhorted Timothy not just to read the Bible but to preach it:

> I charge you in the presence of God and of Christ Jesus, who is to judge the living and the dead, and by his appearing and his kingdom: preach the word; be ready in season and out of season; reprove, rebuke, and exhort, with complete patience and teaching. (2 Tim. 4:1–2)

Reformed churches have a very high view of preaching. They understand that the sermon is not simply a lecture, a teaching event that is more or less equivalent to a university lecture or TED Talk. Nor is it a case of Pastor Nigel speaking to Hill Street Church about Jesus. Rather, Jesus addresses Hill Street through Pastor Nigel.

Of course, this happens only as the minister faithfully expounds on the Bible's message. It is Christ our great prophet who is active. Paul defended himself before Festus by claiming that he was only doing what Moses said would happen—namely, that "Christ must suffer and that, by being the first to rise from the dead, he would proclaim light both to our people and to the Gentiles" (Acts 26:23). Notice it is *Christ* who is doing the proclaiming, not just his servants as they preach about him. Likewise, Paul told the Ephesians, a church in modern-day Turkey that Christ certainly never visited during his earthly ministry, that Jesus "came and preached peace to you" (Eph. 2:17). This preaching was through the missionaries, pastors, and evangelists Christ commissioned.[8]

This high view of preaching is why one Reformed confession is willing to say, "The preaching of the word of God is the word of God."[9] And the Westminster Larger Catechism, having asked in question 155, "How is the Word made effectual to salvation?" answers in part, "The Spirit of God makes the reading, *but especially the preaching of the Word,* an effectual means of enlightening, convincing, and humbling sinners."

In his mercy and wisdom, God has chosen to reach the world through the ordinary preaching of ordinary men. But, in the words of Presbyterian minister and theologian Jonathan Landry Cruse, the sermon is when "Jesus gets up to preach."[10] Preaching is thus less "one beggar telling another where to find bread" and more the King himself giving bread to a beggar, albeit through the hands of another.

God's People Respond: Psalms, Hymns, and Spiritual Songs

By now you've hopefully spotted the pattern. Christ ministers his Word to us in all sorts of different ways. He invites us, calls us to worship, convicts us of sin, comforts us with the gospel, and, through the sermon, corrects us, rebukes us, and encourages us. Each time he speaks, we, the church, respond by speaking back to him. Often that response comes through prayer, and sometimes that prayer is sung.

Paul encourages the Colossians to "let the word of Christ dwell in you richly, teaching and admonishing one another in all wisdom, singing psalms and hymns and spiritual songs, with thankfulness in your hearts to God" (Col. 3:16). God has given the church a hymnbook, the book of Psalms. Reformed churches have differed on the question of whether we should *only* sing scriptural psalms in worship. We'll look at that question in the question and answer section that ends this book. No one denies that we ought to be singing at least some psalms! Yet in many churches the Psalms are all but forgotten, perhaps with the honorable exception of Psalm 23.

The Psalms are a treasure trove for God's people. Almost uniquely in Scripture, they are God's Word given to the church to speak back to him. Reading through the Psalms, you'll also find that there is tremendous variety. There are songs of thanksgiving, songs of lament, songs of praise, songs that are prayers for help, songs of confession of sin—the list could go on. Many of our modern songs tend to revolve around one or two themes and are invariably upbeat. But God's people regularly weep, and the Psalms help to give mourning saints voice.

God Speaks: The Lord's Supper

Remember how the Levitical offerings ended with the peace offering—the one offering that the worshipper and God both "ate" together? Remember how at the end of the covenant ceremony at Sinai, Moses and the elders were invited up the mountain to eat and drink with God? Remember how the whole Bible story is headed toward the wedding supper of the Lamb? Eating is a big deal, and to eat with another person is sign that you are in good fellowship, welcome at each other's table.

The Lord's Supper proclaims just this message to God's people. It is of course a remembrance and the way of "seeing" what Christ has done for us. His words at the Last Supper are significant: "Do *this* in remembrance of me" (Luke 22:19). We have endless books on how to be a gospel-centered parent, preach a gospel-centered sermon, lead a gospel-centered church. Yet many of us also have a low view of the Lord's

Supper, the meal Jesus himself gave us during his last evening on earth to help us to remember the gospel. Communion is Christ's route to gospel centrality.

The bread and wine are therefore "visible words" that preach and personalize the gospel message to Christ's people again. In this sense, the Supper is more about God speaking to us than us remembering him. Calvin writes, "Let it be regarded as a settled principle that the sacraments have the same office as the Word of God: to offer and set forth Christ to us, and in him the treasures of heavenly grace."[11]

The Lord's Supper doesn't only preach to us. It is not only a sign. Just as the Word of God doesn't bring just information but, by the power of the Spirit, unites us to Christ and brings all his riches to us, so too the Supper. Consider Paul's words to the church in Corinth: "The cup of blessing that we bless, is it not a participation in the blood of Christ? The bread that we break, is it not a participation in the body of Christ?" (1 Cor. 10:16). In older versions, the word the ESV translates as "participation" was often "communion," hence *Communion* is another common name for the Lord's Supper. Mysteriously, as we eat and drink, we are, spiritually speaking, feeding on Christ. It's not that the bread and wine transform into his body and blood. Rather, the Holy Spirit takes this ordinary loaf and ordinary cup and uses them to strengthen our communion with Christ.

Is there mystery here? Certainly. Though there's also mystery in the way the Spirit uses light bouncing off the page of a Bible as we read it, passing through our retinas, and sending pulses down our optic nerves to somehow strengthen our faith. God is in the business of using physical things to do us spiritual good. So, alongside a reminder to our eyes, God is giving us grace and strength through our mouths and hands. It is a meal, after all! Just as physical bread and wine strengthen our earthly bodies, so this spiritual bread and wine—Christ himself—strengthen our souls.

There's much more we could say about the Lord's Supper. But we'll close this section with these beautiful words from question 75 of the Heidelberg Catechism. See again that the emphasis is first of all on God's action, his gift to us in the Supper, and only secondarily on our receiving of that gift: "First, as surely as I see with my eyes the bread of the Lord broken for me and the cup given to me, so surely was his body offered for me and his blood poured out for me on the cross. Second, as surely as I receive from the hand of the minister and taste with my mouth the bread and the cup of the Lord as sure signs of Christ's body and blood, so surely does he himself nourish and refresh my soul to everlasting life with his crucified body and shed blood."

God's People Respond: Tithes and Offerings

It is often at this point of the service that we offer our gifts to God in the form of an offering. We have just been reminded that we are one body in the Lord's Supper. In many ways throughout the service, we have heard of God's grace to us. So it's right and natural to want to give to him in thanks, particularly as we give of our abundance to help those in the body who are in need.

> And all who believed were together and had all things in common. And they were selling their possessions and belongings and distributing the proceeds to all, as any had need. (Acts 2:44–45)

> On the first day of every week, each of you is to put something aside and store it up, as he may prosper, so that there will be no collecting when I come. (1 Cor. 16:2)

God Speaks: To Bless and Send Out His People

The worship service ends with a benediction, or blessing. This is not a closing prayer. Prayers are directed from man to God. Blessings are spoken from God to his people. They are a final message from heaven to earth. The classic example of a benediction comes in Numbers 6:

> The Lord spoke to Moses, saying, "Speak to Aaron and his sons, saying, Thus you shall bless the people of Israel: you shall say to them,
>
> > The LORD bless you and keep you;
> > the LORD make his face to shine upon you and be
> > > gracious to you;

> the LORD lift up his countenance upon you and
> give you peace.

"So shall they put my name upon the people of Israel,
and I will bless them." (vv. 22–27)

Aaron & Co. are not praying to God that he might do
these things for the Israelites. Rather they are proclaiming, in God's name, that this is what God will do for his
people. The last phrase is crucial: "And *I* will bless them."
Ultimately the blessing is from God.

The minister most likely raises his hands during the
closing blessing. This is the posture regularly used for benedictions in the Bible (see Lev. 9:22; Ps. 134:2; Luke 24:50).
The idea is similar to that of laying on of hands. When the
great patriarchs blessed their children, they laid hands on
their heads and pronounced the blessing. For Aaron with
the congregation of Israel—or for that matter your pastor
with the congregation gathered next Sunday—laying hands
on each person's head was impossible. So instead a minister
raises his hands over all God's people as he pronounces
the blessing.

Hear the words as coming from Christ. You leave with
his name upon you, with a final reminder of the peace you
enjoy: the favor and blessing of God that rest upon you.
This is not a time to close your eyes and look down. Rather,
lift your head and look to see Christ ministering his Word
to you one more time.

Only then, with the blessing ringing in your ears, will your pastor dismiss you with some appropriate words: "Let us go in peace to love and serve the Lord." Worship has concluded, and we head out to serve.

Christ from Every Angle

The gospel-structured service is designed to help us to meet Christ from every angle. Someone who wants to grow in appreciation of Handel's music goes to a concert; a devotee of Rembrandt goes to an art gallery. They don't go there and then focus on how good a job they're doing of listening to the music or looking at the art. Likewise, in worship we look primarily to Christ to have faith drawn out of us, rather than concentrate on how much we're enjoying the service or how well we're listening. *He* calls us, *he* convicts us, *he* comforts us, *he* receives our prayers, *he* addresses us in the reading and sermon, *he* invites us to his table and feeds us there, *he* blesses us and sends us out into his world. At each stage, our primary duty is to receive, empty handed. Martin Luther's dying words say it all: "We are beggars; this is true." Thankfully, our God is the God of beggars.

Questions for Further Reflection

1. Why might a "gospel-shaped" service help us to meet Christ in all his fullness?

2. How does the idea of worship as a dialogue help us on Sundays?
3. How does a Reformed understanding of preaching help us to understand why the sermon is longer than the Bible readings on a Sunday?
4. Having read this book, what might you change in your approach to next Sunday?

QUESTIONS AND ANSWERS ON REFORMED WORSHIP

There is perhaps no area of church life more debated than that of worship! Even among Bible-believing, God-honoring Christians who advocate a Reformed approach to worship, there is debate on some (though not all!) of the questions below. I submit these not as "final answers" but in the hope that they will be of service to God's people as they engage in the conversation.

The Time and Place of Worship

Isn't all of life worship?

In one sense, yes, this is true. Having spent eleven chapters explaining all that God has done for his people in the gospel, Paul begins Romans 12 by telling the church, "Present your bodies as a living sacrifice, holy and acceptable to God, which is your spiritual worship" (Rom. 12:1). What will this spiritual worship look like? The focus in the following verses is not on a worship service but rather on the transformed life the Christian is called to live. Paul speaks of humility, love, submission to earthly rulers, feeding the hungry, and so on. Similarly, some of the words occasionally translated *worship* in modern English translations of the Old Testament refer to general all-of-life service of God.

But this doesn't mean that there aren't times when people gather for focused worship of the Lord. The Psalms are full of calls to *begin* worshipping God: "Oh come, let us worship and bow down; let us kneel before the LORD, our Maker!" (Ps. 95:6). Zechariah speaks of those who "shall go up year after year to worship the King, the LORD of hosts" (Zech. 14:16). When the magi, the wise men, came to Jesus's house, "they fell down and worshiped him" (Matt. 2:11). It is "while they were worshiping the Lord and fasting" that the church in Antioch received a prophecy about sending Paul (see Acts 13:2). When the elders in heaven heard the earth sing the Lamb's praises, they "fell down and worshiped" (Rev. 5:14). Each of these passages, and many dozens more, describe worship as an activity we're invited to begin or as something God's people did at a certain time. If the only sense of worship was "all of life," then none of them would make any sense. All Christians would be worshipping, nonstop, all the time! As this book has argued, there are set times of "corporate worship" that are marked off from the rest of life.

Does it matter what day we meet?

Yes. The "Lord's day" (Rev. 1:10) is the first day of the week: Sunday. This is the day God appointed to gather his children before him in worship. Ever since the creation of the world, God has set aside one day for a "sabbath," a day *of* rest and *for* God. Of course, we can worship God on our own or with our families at any time. Similarly, we may be part of a church small group or midweek prayer meeting. In each of these settings, we draw near to God. But there is something special about meeting with God's people on the day he appointed and called them together to meet with him through the channels he has given.

Should we celebrate Christmas, Easter, and the church calendar?

Since the day Christ ascended to heaven, the church has celebrated several "feast days." Often these days are tied to a great event in God's salvation plan: Christ's birth (Christmas), death (Good Friday), resurrection (Easter Sunday), and so on. Although the truths these days celebrate are clearly biblical, the Bible itself doesn't command their celebration on a particular day. During the old covenant, there were three main (and several smaller) festivals that God's people were commanded to keep. Nowadays, in the era of the new covenant, the only special day is the Sabbath.

That means a church may decide they'd like to celebrate the incarnation at Christmas. But, assuming that day is not a Sunday, the church elders would not be able to "bind the conscience" of church members in insisting they attend the service. Again, see the freeing nature of the regulative principle! Church ministers have no authority beyond that of Scripture—their authority is ministerial and declarative. It is *ministerial* in that they serve in the name and authority of another, Christ. A minister is simply a servant. And it is *declarative* in that they have authority only to declare what Christ has legislated in his Word. This doesn't include dozens of holy days.

In some church traditions, almost every day of the year has some special meaning or way it may be celebrated. Christ doesn't bind us in this way! But if you want to gather to celebrate Christmas as a family, or if your elders decide they'll hold a (nonbinding!) Good Friday service, then few Reformed Christians will complain!

Is gathered worship more important than my personal worship?

There's a section of the evangelical church that would immediately say, "No, of course not. What matters most are your personal times of prayer and Bible reading." Perhaps it's a symptom of our increasingly individualistic society, but we have a tendency to prioritize the personal over the corporate.

It seems, however, that Scripture leans the other way. Not, of course, that personal prayer is unimportant! But the chief means of grace through which God blesses his people are those found in the corporate gathering of the church: the preached Word and the sacraments. After all, for most of history the only way people could encounter the Word was when it was read to them: people neither owned Bibles nor could read. Likewise, when we meet corporately, we are not turning up only for our own spiritual benefit but also for that of our brothers and sisters. Instead of asking, "What did I get out of this?" as we leave a worship service, we could enjoy far healthier Sundays if we asked, "How did I glorify God and serve my neighbor?"

The author of Hebrews writes, "Let us consider how to stir up one another to love and good works, not neglecting to meet together, as is the habit of some, but encouraging one another" (Heb. 10:24–25). See how the author couples "meeting together" (the "synagogue-ing" verb again: this is church, not a small group) with a focus on one another.

So personal and family worship are great blessings, but neither is to be privileged over the Sunday gathering.

Can I stay home and worship with my family?

Although family and personal worship are great blessings, they are not to be used as a substitute for corporate worship. God calls his whole church together—men, women, and children—each Sunday to minister to them through the officers he has appointed (see Eph. 4:8–13). We have no right to refuse the invitation or set up our own alternative "in house." The church and the family are different institutions, both created and blessed by God but fulfilling different callings. The church is a gathering of God's people that crosses biological family lines. The ministry of Word and sacrament is the responsibility of the church.

Similarly, staying home and watching a worship service online cannot be an adequate substitute. Of course, in emergency situations, such as an illness, it may be the best we can manage. But worship is what happens when the church comes together. We are physical beings, so that gathering involves our bodies. Think, for example, of the Lord's Supper, a physical meal in which we share one loaf. There is no way of doing this other than in the gathered church. The sacraments are given by Jesus to the church, not to the individual or family.

Does corporate worship only occur in a church building?

No. With the move from the old covenant to the new, there are no more "holy places" on earth. The temple in which God dwells is not a temple of bricks and mortar but rather the temple of the people of God. As you watch people file through the door on Sunday morning, it is not that they have arrived at church. Rather, church has arrived at the building!

Isn't worship just the singing part of the service?

Singing is one of the things the church does to worship God, but it's not the entirety of worship. To sing praise to God and to worship are not synonyms. Even at the level of the New Testament "worship" words, this should be obvious. In Revelation we read that "the twenty-four elders fall down before him who is seated on the throne and worship him who lives forever and ever. They cast their crowns before the throne, *saying . . .*" (Rev. 4:10). *Saying*, not singing! When the magi worshipped the infant Jesus, when the disciples in the boat worshipped the Jesus who stilled the storm, when the blind man worshipped the Jesus who gave him sight, it's hard to believe each person was breaking into song!

Singing is a great gift, but we shouldn't divide a church service into worship (singing) and other things. When we gather on Sunday, we worship as we pray, as we listen to God's Word, as we give, as we come to the Lord's Table, and so on.

Worship Practices

Why don't you speak in tongues and prophesy?

Reformed Christians understand New Testament prophecy to be fundamentally the same as Old Testament prophecy: it is the Word of God. That's why when a prophet spoke in the New Testament, he began, "Thus says the Holy Spirit . . . ," just as Old Testament prophets began, "Thus says the LORD" (Acts 21:11). Prophecy is never "I get the feeling God *might* be saying . . ." or "I have a sense that . . ." or "I'm being given a picture of . . ." No, prophets in the New Testament are described as laying the foundation of the church, along with the apostles, as they speak and write the very Word of God (see Eph. 2:20).

Now that God's Word is written and complete, there is no longer a need for new revelation (see 2 Tim. 3:16; Heb. 1:1–2). Prophecy therefore has ceased, as has the role of apostle. When Paul describes Timothy as a "man of God," he is applying an Old Testament term for a prophet to the ordinary pastor. But this "man of God" is not going to receive new revelation (like a prophet). Instead, Paul commands him to "preach the word"—the Word the prophets have already given (see 2 Tim 3:16–4:2).

"Tongues" are in the same category: someone speaking in tongues is giving a prophecy but in a different (and, to them, unlearned) language—the word *tongue* is a perfectly normal word for a language (see 1 Cor 14:3–5; see also Acts 2:1–11).

Given that prophecy—new revelation of the binding, authoritative Word of God—has ceased, so have the gifts of being an apostle, a prophet, or a prophetic tongue-speaker.

Why do we say creeds?

Many (though not all) Reformed churches recite the creeds of the church in worship services. The role of the creeds is threefold. First, they are a means of teaching: as we recite the Nicene Creed, for example, we are being taught orthodox Trinitarian theology. Second, they are a form of response to God's Word. The Word is preached, and we worship God by proclaiming, "We believe . . ."

Finally, the creeds are gatekeepers: they function as summaries of what Christians are to believe if they are to be members of Christ's church.

Almost all heretics claim to be following Scripture. But Scripture can be distorted and wrongly taught. Hence, when Paul instructs Timothy to "follow the pattern of the sound words that you have heard from me" (2 Tim. 1:13) and "guard the good deposit entrusted to you" (2 Tim. 1:14), he is instructing Timothy not so much to keep the text of Scripture pure but to protect and pass on its correct interpretation. Creeds help with this guarding and proclaiming work. They serve as a reminder that Reformed believers are not seeking to be sectarian, believing they are the only "true Christians" on earth. Rather, we are part of a wider family, stretched across the continents and down through the ages, who together profess the faith summarized in the creeds.

Is reading "set prayers" in a worship service unspiritual?

In the Old Testament, God gave 150 psalms as set prayers or songs for his people. These were largely designed for corporate worship. When the disciples asked Jesus how they should pray, he taught them the prayer we now know as the Lord's Prayer. It is, of course, possible to switch off and repeat a psalm or prayer with no engagement of head or heart. But that is the fault of our heads and hearts, not the prayer! Particularly in corporate worship, it is beautiful to hear the congregation praying together as one. For this to happen, there needs to be agreement on the words to be prayed.

Corporate prayers can also train us to pray when we're alone or worshipping with our families. The Psalms, for example, tend to be more extensive in their range of petitions and prayers than many of us would naturally be on our own. A healthy prayer life can be "caught" as much as "taught" when we pray them.

It may also be worth adding that Christians who have a problem with saying set prayers rarely have a problem with singing "set songs" off a screen. But most of these songs are just prayers set to music. Speaking rather than singing doesn't make them any less spiritual.

Why do we confess our sin if we're already forgiven?

The moment someone turns to Christ in faith, that person is justified and at peace with God. So when we confess our sins, we are not "becoming Christians again." Nor are we returning to a "state of grace," as if, had we died before we had confessed, we would not have been saved. No, all who trust Christ are safe: "There is therefore now no condemnation for those who are in Christ Jesus" (Rom. 8:1).

Although the penalty of sin no longer hangs over us, the presence of sin remains. We confess because we are part of a covenant people, and God is our God. When we sin against him, it is right for us to acknowledge this and ask his forgiveness. We do so with humble confidence, knowing that he has promised to forgive.

When we fail to confess and persist in sin, our Father may discipline us. To give just one example from Scripture, David experienced exactly this sin-discipline-confession-forgiveness dynamic:

> For when I kept silent, my bones wasted away
>   through my groaning all day long.
> For day and night your hand was heavy upon me;
>   my strength was dried up as by the heat of summer.
>
> I acknowledged my sin to you,
>   and I did not cover my iniquity;
> I said, "I will confess my transgressions to the LORD,"
>   and you forgave the iniquity of my sin. (Ps. 32:3–5)

Why do pastors and elders do so much in a service?

The pastor is not a priest, a mediator between Christ and his people. But he is an appointed shepherd, a preacher and teacher of God's Word. Not everyone holds that position, and not everyone has the gifts and responsibilities of leading and teaching God's people (see Eph. 4:11–12; 1 Tim. 3:1–7). So although the Bible teaches the "priesthood of all believers," which means each Christian has direct access to God through Christ (see 1 Peter 2:9), this is not the same as saying that all Christians are elders in God's church. It is the pastor-teacher who is instructed to read and preach the Bible to God's people (see 1 Tim. 4:13) and to lead the flock.

The pastor is ministering the Word throughout the service, not just in the sermon. He bears this responsibility as much when he is calling the church to confess their sins, inviting them to the Lord's Table, or pronouncing the benediction as he does when he's preaching on the passage for that week.

Should children be in the main service?

One of the things that often surprises visitors to Presbyterian or more broadly Reformed churches is that children are typically present in the worship service rather than being dismissed to special children's groups or gathering separately for "children's church." The idea behind this is that children are as much a part of the congregation as adults. They are not "the future of the church"; they *are* the church, just as much as their parents.

Worship is the gathering of God's covenant people to meet him. Throughout Scripture, the children of believers are included in that people. That's why Abraham was told to circumcise his sons on the eighth day and why Israelite children grew up under the laws of Israel: they didn't grow up neutral and then decide on their sixteenth birthday whether they'd like to keep the Sabbath, abstain from pork, and gather to worship Yahweh. When the prophet Joel called God's people to assemble, he spelled this out explicitly: "Blow the trumpet in Zion; consecrate a fast;

call a solemn assembly; gather the people. Consecrate the congregation; assemble the elders; gather the children, even nursing infants" (Joel 2:15–16). When we come to the New Testament, children remain members of the covenant community. It is therefore assumed they are part of the church's main gathering. That's why Paul addresses them directly in his letters, which were read when the church assembled (see Eph. 6:1–3; Col. 3:20).

If the main way God blesses his people is through the means of grace, especially the preached Word, then it makes sense for us to want our children to experience the means of grace as well! They grow up learning how to worship as they see their parents and older brothers and sisters in the Lord worshipping week by week. It's a tremendous blessing for them to be a part of the worshipping community from their earliest days. They won't understand everything all the time, and that's fine. No one teaches us how to speak our native language; we grow up into it and pick it up. So too we learn the language of worship.

Sacraments

How often should we celebrate the Lord's Supper?

The Bible has no clear instructions on this question. Ministers and elders therefore reason from the purpose of the Supper as to how frequently we should take it. Many— among whom we might count John Calvin—advocate weekly celebration. After all, if it is one of the chief means of grace, why would we not want to put ourselves in the way of God's blessing as often as possible? Then there's the pattern of celebratory meals we saw earlier, in which God's eating and drinking with his people is, in one sense at least, the high point of the whole service.

Others have put more weight on the seriousness of the meal and therefore the need for self-examination in preparation (see 1 Cor. 11:27–30). Indeed, some Scottish churches celebrated the Lord's Supper annually, building up to a "communion season," to allow for this.

Although there is no set pattern, given that the Lord Jesus commanded us to "do *this* in remembrance of me," it would seem that we should celebrate the Supper fairly frequently.

Should children take the Lord's Supper?

No. Or rather—not until they're ready. Sometimes people reason that if children are members of the covenant community, the church (which they are), and therefore have the right to the entry sign, baptism (which they do), then surely they should automatically be allowed to take Communion as well. This is skewed thinking. The two signs are related but distinct. On the one hand, baptism is passive: you do not "take baptism," you are baptized. It is a sign, among other things, of the triune God putting his name on you. Infants need to profess no faith in order to receive this sign; it is theirs by right of being born into the covenant family. The Lord's Supper, on the other hand, is active. We take, eat, drink, feed. It is the sign not of entry but of "going on," a spiritual feeding. And so Paul gives certain "qualifications" as to who should partake:

> Whoever, therefore, eats the bread or drinks the cup of the Lord in an unworthy manner will be guilty concerning the body and blood of the Lord. Let a person examine himself, then, and so eat of the bread and drink of the cup. For anyone who eats and drinks without discerning the body eats and drinks judgment on himself. (1 Cor. 11:27–29)

Those taking the Supper must not do so in an "unworthy manner." This implies that, unlike baptism, we are active in how we receive the sacrament and could do so wrongly. Therefore we must "examine" ourselves before eating and drinking. At the very least, this requires people to have the ability to acknowledge that they are trusting in Christ. Participants also need to "discern the body." This phrase has caused no small debate, but for our purposes we need only note that again it requires thought and judgment. All these acts require a certain maturity.

Question and answer 81 of the Heidelberg Catechism put it like this: "Who are to come to the table of the Lord? Those who are displeased with themselves for their sins, yet trust that these are forgiven them, and that their remaining infirmity is covered by the passion and death of Christ; who also desire more and more to strengthen their faith and to amend their life. But the impenitent and hypocrites eat and drink judgment to themselves."

As to at what age a child can make a "credible profession of faith" and be admitted to the Lord's Table, that depends on the judgment of the parents and ultimately the church elders who oversee the flock.

Is baptism properly observed in a worship service?

Baptism is the "entry sign" to the new covenant people of God, the church. In particular, it is the marker of the visible church, and therefore it is quite proper to conduct baptisms in the context of the weekly gathering of that church.

Regulative Principle

On what principles do you make decisions on the "circumstances" of worship?

Even the staunchest advocate of the regulative principle believes that some of the "how" questions are left to the wisdom of church leaders. Decisions on how long to preach, how many songs to sing, what version of the Bible to preach from, and so on are not questions that can be *directly* answered by appeal to a Bible text.

There are, though, certain principles that we try to apply. Among these is the idea that worship should be edifying and should build up the congregation, a central theme of 1 Corinthians 14. Linked to this, we should work to make things as simple as possible for people to understand. Then there's Paul's command that "all things should be done decently and in order," not least because "God is not a God of confusion but of peace" (1 Cor. 14:40, 33). Services are not more spiritual for being more spontaneous—or indeed chaotic!

Many of these principles are outworkings of the great command to love one another and put others before ourselves. Those who lead worship should seek to make it as simple and straightforward as possible for the congregation to meet with their God.

Isn't the regulative principle very restrictive?

In one sense, yes—but not all restrictions are bad! I once worked at a school whose sports fields were right on the cliff tops. Unsurprisingly, they had a fence around their edge. The fence stopped kids from toppling into the sea—and so I suppose it restricted their freedom in a way. But really the fence freed them to be able to play rugby, cricket, and football without fear or danger.

A Reformed approach to worship sets us free from displeasing God and from the daft or even downright idolatrous ideas of the minister. In the days of the Reformation, the principle developed in response to the Roman Catholic church's invention of all sorts of rites and ceremonies that deviated from the Word of God. Protestant congregations were freed from the need to kiss the images of saints, cross themselves before an "altar," celebrate endless holy days, and so on. A Reformed approach to worship is simple and freeing!

Isn't Reformed worship a Western approach to worship?

If it originates in Scripture, a better critique would be that it's a Middle Eastern approach! We mustn't mix up "elements" and "circumstances." There are differences in what a Reformed worship service looks like in Jakarta, Mombasa, Dublin, and Denver. The differences may include areas such as the style of preaching and praying and likely the kinds of music, among other things. But at their core the Word and sacrament will be central—they are God's means of meeting people of every tribe, tongue, and nation in the context of their own culture.

Should we sing only psalms?

The view that we should sing only psalms in worship has been the position of several Reformed theologians and denominations down the centuries. *Exclusive psalmody*, as this position is known, has many strong arguments in its favor. Advocates look to Paul's command to sing "psalms, hymns, and spiritual songs" and point out that these three categories map onto the "superscriptions" of various of the psalms in the book of Psalms. "Where," they ask, "is the warrant for non-scriptural songs?"

On the other side are those who see singing not so much as an "element" of worship itself but rather as one form of prayer or teaching. As we praise God in the words of hymns like "Holy, Holy, Holy" or ask his blessing in "Guide Me, O Thou Great Jehovah," we are not doing anything fundamentally different than when we come before him in the prayers of intercession, invocation, or adoration. No one thinks these prayers need to be restricted to readings of Scripture. Worship is a dialogue. So singing prayers, praises, and petitions is a valid way of responding to God.

Of course both "sides" would agree that the content of any song (or indeed prayer) ought to be thoroughly biblical.

What about showing videos in worship?

There may be some differences of opinion here among those who hold to a Reformed view of worship. Including clips from movies and TV shows is unlikely to be helpful and seems to me to be introducing a whole new "element" into the service. A video update from a missionary, followed by prayer for them, may be seen by one congregation as a valid example of "encouraging one another" and by another as an unnecessary interruption of worship. We need to be generous with one another! But we do want to resist the move from Word to image: God has given us a book, not a movie, and he has not made a mistake. Christianity is, for now, primarily a religion of the ear rather than the eye—the sacraments being the one exception. We live by faith, not by sight, and God's method of reaching and teaching the world is through the preached Word.

Worship Concerns

Aren't your services a bit formal and boring?

The ordered nature of a Reformed service is a reflection of our God, who "is not a God of confusion but of peace" (1 Cor. 14:33). That's why Paul could tell genuine prophets who received revelations from God to sit down and wait their turn—or even not to speak at all if two or three had already done so (see 1 Cor. 14:28–33).

The liturgy also helps the congregation to worship together. A friend was once at a service in which the music leader stood up, read Psalm 33:3 ("Sing to him a new song"), and announced we would do just that. But as it was new, it was up to each person to make it up as they went along. Unsurprisingly, chaos ensued, as even the musicians played different tunes in different keys! The liturgy functions like the rules of basketball: rather than restricting the players, it enables them to all join in and benefit.

As for boring, meeting with God should never be boring! But we are not coming to be entertained or titillated. Fun is not a spiritual virtue. We are meeting with the Lord of the universe. "Let us offer to God acceptable worship, with reverence and awe, for our God is a consuming fire," wrote the author of Hebrews (Heb. 12:28–29). Boredom is not an aim either! But a right seriousness about worship is not the same thing as being dull. "Serve the LORD with fear, and rejoice with trembling," says the psalmist (Ps. 2:11). As we saw earlier, fear and joy are not mutually exclusive.

When we gather, we come not just into the presence of those we can see but also into the presence of "innumerable angels in festal gathering, and to the assembly of the first-born who are enrolled in heaven, and to God, the judge of all, and to the spirits of the righteous made perfect, and to Jesus" (Heb. 12:22–24). So we ought to ask whether we'd act in the way we are if we could *see* the flaming cherubim in the third row. Or still more, if we could see the Lord Jesus enthroned at the front of the room. We can't see them—but they are there. The tone of a worship service ought to reflect this.

Shouldn't we be creative in worship?

There is a lot of freedom in new covenant worship. The regulative principle doesn't lead to cookie-cutter services that all look the same world over. Certainly we should be thoughtful about the songs we sing, the ordering of the service, the sermons we preach, the prayers we pray, and so on. But we're not called to be creative in finding new ways to meet with God. It is up to him to decide by what means Christ meets with us.

Nor are we to be creative in some misguided attempt to keep people entertained. Imagine the Israelites as Passover approached yet again. "Yes, there was the death of the firstborn, but that wasn't the only plague," says one. "Passover is getting repetitive. This year, why don't we get creative and dye all our water red to remind us of the Nile turning to blood. In fact, while we're at it, since God is the Creator, why don't we each create something and bring it to the tabernacle as an offering this Sabbath? And for that matter, Aaron, the kids are finding the same old Day of Atonement rituals so dull. You're risking losing them. Can't you find your funniest priest and get him to do something more engaging this year—perhaps a puppet show? At the very least he could dress up as Pharaoh and we could throw frogs at him?"

I realize there's a risk this sounds facetious—but we worship *exactly* the same God as did Moses, Aaron, David, and Solomon. Joy, reverence, and awe are comfortable bedfellows. They sit less well with triviality and banality. It is a seriously joyful thing to meet with the living God.

Why not make worship more like a small-group question and answer time?

Although many believers have benefited from small-group Bible discussions, these are not the same thing as the church gathered to worship. We meet at God's call on the Lord's Day and are addressed by him through his Word in the hand of his ministers. This Word is not up for question or debate: our covenant Lord is speaking to us. The method—preaching—fits the message: the gospel (see 1 Cor. 1:18–21). Both emphasize that this is good news from heaven, not advice that is up for discussion. Hence, there is a pattern in Scripture of prophets and preachers alike—not least the Lord Jesus himself—giving "monologues" when preaching (see Luke 4:16–21; see also 2 Tim. 4:2).

There is, of course, a place for talking through what we've heard in the service and sermon, and any sensible pastor is delighted to answer questions that congregation members have about the Word he has preached. But these questions should come after the worship service itself has concluded.

Should we make worship "accessible" for non-Christians?

Worship is about God's people coming to meet with him. The focus is first and foremost on him and on doing the things that please him. The focus is second on God's people, the church. Those planning worship are guided by the knowledge that this is the high point of the week, the chief way God blesses and builds his church. We can't afford to mess about with the worship service in order to turn it into an evangelistic event. That would be like making a wedding more accessible to lonely hearts and singles by not having a bride and groom.

Having said that, we do hope that non-Christians will come along. More than that, worship is the best event to invite them along to! Paul envisages a non-Christian coming in, seeing the church at worship, and falling down in awe (see 1 Cor. 14:24–25). This makes sense if worship is the place and time where God and his people meet.

As a student, I finally convinced a non-Christian friend to come to church, only to sit cringing when the preacher got up to speak on Paul's instructions to married couples in

Ephesians 5. I spent most of the sermon thinking through how to persuade my friend to come back next week. But my fears were misplaced: my friend was gripped and never stopped coming back! In the context of the worshipping church, God's preached Word had met him in power. For that matter, for many in the West, a church service is probably a less weird thing to visit than a quiz night or golf day with an evangelistic talk: at least in a church service they are expecting "religious stuff," and it's naturally on the agenda.

Worshipping Well

How should I prepare for worship?

To begin with practical matters, preparation for Sunday morning begins on Saturday night. Culturally (in the West, at least), this is often a night for staying up late, especially for younger folk in the church. But if we're up to all hours on Saturday, we're likely to be not just physically but spiritually sleepy on Sunday. Just as we'd try to get a good night's sleep if we knew we had an important exam or interview the next day, so all the more should we be well rested to meet with our God.

Likewise, arriving early, getting settled, and taking some time to prepare your heart and mind before the call to worship will also help you engage. Of course, there are times when the latter in particular is hard, especially if you're looking after a gaggle of young children. Flustered mums should be encouraged to remember they're coming to a Savior who welcomed the little children to him and no doubt can sympathize with exhausted and somewhat frazzled parents. But in general we ought to arrive not as the service begins, or one minute beforehand, but with enough time to spare to settle.

Then, as addressed in the answer to the previous question, we should do all we can to prepare ourselves spiritually. Lots of churches send out the order of service, or at least the passage to be preached, in advance. It can help to practice songs with children in advance and talk through the Scripture reading. And, most significantly of all, we come before the Lord in prayer, like the beggars of his own day: empty handed, simply asking for blessing that we know we do not deserve, but that he in his grace loves to give.

Does it matter what I wear to worship?

No, not really. As ever, Christians want to dress modestly and appropriately. Cultures vary widely on matters of clothing. Some Christians want to be at the "smarter" end of their culture's dress codes when they gather in the Lord's presence. But this is an area of freedom where we should show grace to one another.

What if I don't feel like worshipping?

The Christian life is not one of uninterrupted ecstasy and euphoria. There are times when we come to church weeping at the tragedies of life. There are times when we are weighed down by the guilt and burden of our sin. There are times, frankly, when God feels distant, his face somehow hidden (see Psalm 88 for one example). At these times, we need to cling to God's promise and hear Christ's invitation, "Come to me, all who labor and are heavy laden, and I will give you rest" (Matt. 11:28). We must remember that our feelings and experiences are not the measure of whether or not we've met with God. His Word always does its work, whatever the ups and downs of our emotions or spiritual experience.

A word too on singing. Whether your church sings only psalms, or whether you sing hymns as well, there are times when you don't *feel* the same as the psalmist or hymn writer. In fact, if you were to pick four or five psalms to sing more or less at random, you'd almost certainly find a host of seemingly contradictory "experiences" being expressed. One moment we're declaring, "My whole being rejoices" (Ps. 16:9); the next, "My soul is cast down within me" (Ps. 42:6). Should we sing only if we feel the same way? No. We can join in with the congregation, recognizing first that we sing in harmony with brothers and sisters who *are* feeling that way, whether in our own congregation or in the wider church. Second, we sing the Psalms as words to grow into. We *want* to be people who can sing, "I love the Lord" (Ps. 116:1), even if we don't *feel* full of love at that moment.

The Psalms function as a way of learning the full range of biblical emotions and how to express them. Just as we teach our children to say thank you even when we're not entirely sure they feel it, as a way of training them to be thankful, so too we sing to become more like the psalmists.[1] This is not to condone hypocrisy or empty worship. Rather, it is to encourage broken saints who wish they had the passion of David.

What if the worship service is led badly?

We've all had the experience of losing track of the sermon, wondering if a prayer will ever end, being distracted by a screaming baby. For all sorts of reasons—some of them blameworthy, some not—those who lead worship will not always meet our expectations and hopes. Sometimes, to be blunt, worship can feel a slog. But our goal should be to look past the rambling pastor or mumbling pray-er to the Lord behind him. If the preacher is being faithful to Scripture, Christ is speaking to us.

Hopefully there will be something in each sermon, even if we perhaps have to dig a little harder than we'd like.

The more we mature, the easier it becomes for us to be edified. Our ears will be sharper to our need and to Christ's riches on offer. At the end of the day, it's not slick performance that brings power or rather brings Christ: it is his Word carried by his Spirit. So as long as the gospel is central, there ought to be food enough to sustain us.

We need to take care not to sit in judgment over sermons and worship, spending more energy assessing the ministry (and minister) than seeking Christ's grace for ourselves. A good marker of our attitude is how seriously we pray for those shepherding us.

How might I stay more focused in worship?

It helps to remember what "more focused" really means. Our aim is not to be more focused on our experience, our education, or our enjoyment but on the one who is at the center of worship: God the Father, Son, and Holy Spirit. Before you arrive to worship, pray that God would allow you to lift your eyes to him. Whatever is going on in the service, it is primarily God ministering to you: "What has he got to say to me in this sermon? How is he going to comfort me today in the words of assurance?" We should keep our attention on him and on what he is doing rather than how we're finding the service: "What do I think of this new preacher? I never like this hymn. Why is Mike singing so badly?"

If you find your mind has wandered or you've become distracted, rather than spiraling into despair, thank the Holy Spirit for waking you up, quickly repent, rejoice in Christ's grace, and get going again!

Very practically, it helps to remove competitors for your attention. In our day, the primary distraction is likely to be your phone. Switching it off and using a paper Bible hugely reduces the temptations that draw your mind elsewhere.

RECOMMENDED RESOURCES

Introductory

Cruse, Jonathan Landry. *What Happens When We Worship*. Grand Rapids, Reformation Heritage Books, 2020. [A short, highly readable introduction to the elements and pattern of a classic Reformed worship service. Engagingly written by a pastor seeking to introduce Reformed worship to newcomers.]

Chapell, Bryan. *Christ-Centered Worship: Letting the Gospel Shape Our Practice*. Grand Rapids, Baker Academic, 2009. [Although not attempting to argue for an explicitly Reformed view of worship, Chapell has many helpful insights into the history of worship and advice on how to make the gospel the driving force of the service. He also gives examples of liturgies from the ancient, Reformation, and modern church and suggestions for Bible texts that serve the various stages of worship.]

Intermediate

Horton, Michael. *A Better Way: Recovering the Drama of God-Centered Worship*. Baker Book House, 2003. [Horton dives deeper than

Cruse to give more of the underlying theology that underpins an understanding of worship as "dialogue." He also explores the significance of covenant theology in shaping worship.]

Ryken, Philip Graham; Derek W. H. Thomas; J. Ligon Duncan, eds. *Give Praise to God: A Vision for Reforming Worship, Celebrating the Legacy of James Montgomery Boice.* Phillipsburg, P&R Publishing, 2003. [A collection of essays from pastors and scholars committed to Reformed worship. The chapters by Duncan giving biblical evidence for the regulative principle are particularly helpful, as is Thomas's chapter answering common objections.]

Advanced

Bannerman, James. *The Church of Christ.* Edinburgh, The Banner of Truth Trust, 2014. [Written nearly 150 years ago, this is a thorough account of the doctrine of the church with lengthy sections on worship and the sacraments.]

Gibson, Jonathan and Mark Earngey, eds. *Reformation Worship: Liturgies from the Past for the Present.* Greensboro, New Growth Press, 2018. [A large, single-volume collection of liturgies from various Reformed churches, of particular use to those planning worship. Also includes valuable introductory essays on the biblical theology of worship.]

NOTES

Foreword

1 David E. Garland, *1 Corinthians*, Baker Exegetical Commentary on the New Testament (Grand Rapids: Baker Academic, 2003), 674.

Introduction: Welcome In

1 John Calvin, "The Necessity of Reforming the Church," https://www.monergism.com/thethreshold/sdg/calvin_necessityreform.html. Emphasis mine.

Chapter 1: The Promise of Worship

1 David Peterson, *Engaging with God* (Leicester, UK: Apollos, 1992).

2 For a fuller description of the links between Eden and the temple, see Gregory K. Beale, *The Temple and the Church's Mission* (Downers Grove: InterVarsity Press, 2004).

3 For this reading of Exodus, and the understanding of Leviticus that follows, see L. Michael Morales, *Who Shall Ascend the Mountain of the Lord?* (Leicester, UK: Apollos, 2015).

Chapter 2: The Purpose of Worship

1 C. S. Lewis, *Mere Christianity* (London, UK: HarperCollins, 2002), 143.

2 For one translation of this prayer, originally written in German, see *Luther's Prayers*, ed. Herbert. F. Brokering (Augsburg Fortress, Minneapolis, 1994), 67–68.

3 John Jefferson Davis, *Worship and the Reality of God: An Evangelical Theology of Real Presence* (Downers Grove: InterVarsity Press, 2010).

Chapter 3: The Principle of Worship

1 Examples of this can be found all over the Old Testament. Whatever the specifics of the issues, Cain's offering was not acceptable to God and Abel's was. When the Israelites built the golden calf, they were attempting to worship Yahweh (Ex. 32:5), not Baal or Osiris.

2 Although you should consult the laws of your country on whether it is *legal* to do so!

3 The actual phrase *regulative principle* may be relatively modern. Debate over when exactly it was first used is beyond our remit, but the important point is that the *principle* was there, whatever name was given to it.

4 Westminster Confession of Faith, chapter 21.1.

5 Westminster Shorter Catechism, answer 88.

Chapter 4: The Power and Pillars of Worship

1 See Christopher Ash, *Remaking a Broken World* (Milton Keynes, UK: Authentic Media Ltd, 2010), 141.

2 For more on this understanding of apostles and prophets, together with a great introduction to a Reformed understanding of the work of the Spirit, see Sinclair B. Ferguson, *The Holy Spirit* (Nottingham, UK: IVP, 1996).

3 In fact, *Presbyterian* comes from the Greek word meaning "elder." For example, in 1 Timothy 4:14 Paul speaks of the "council of elders." The Greek word is *presbuteriou*, a form of the noun *presbuterion*.

4 John Calvin, *Institutes of the Christian Religion,* ed. John T. McNeill, trans. Ford Lewis Battles (London: Westminster John Knox Press), 4.1.5.

5 See *The Complete Works of John Owen*, vol. 3, *The Holy Spirit* (Carlisle, PA: Banner of Truth, 1966), 192.

6 Herman Bavinck, *Reformed Dogmatics,* ed. John Bolt, trans. John Vriend (Grand Rapids: Baker Academic, 2008), 4:457.

7 Ligon Duncan, *Does God Care How We Worship?* (Phillipsburg, NJ: P&R Publishing, 2020), 77.

8 Westminster Confession of Faith, chapter 21.5.

9 Deuteronomy 6:13; Nehemiah 10:29; Esther 4:16; 9:22; Psalm 107; Ecclesiastes 5:4–5; Isaiah 19:21; 66:2; Joel 2:12; Matthew 9:15; 13:19; 28:19; Acts 2:42; 10:33; 15:21; 1 Corinthians 7:5; 11:23–29; Ephesians 5:19; Colossians 3:16; 2 Timothy 4:2; Hebrews 4:2; 12:28; James 1:22; 5:13; Revelation 1:3.

Chapter 5: The Pattern of Worship

1 Bryan Chapell, *Christ-Centered Worship* (Grand Rapids: Baker Academic, 2009), 15.

2 This is not to say that Jesus never appeared to anyone on any day other than Sunday. Rather, we see that whenever a specific day is mentioned, it's the first day. This can't be a coincidence!

3 For more on Sabbath, including a discussion of the idea that Sabbath is just an old covenant reality, see Thomas Witherow, *I Will Build My Church: Selected Writings on Church Polity, Baptism, and Sabbath*, ed. Jonathan Gibson (Glenside, PA: Westminster Seminary Press, 2022).

4 For the first appearance of this order, see Leviticus 9. But you'll spot the pattern all over the Old Testament once you grasp it! For the offerings themselves, read Leviticus 1–5, which explains the purpose of each.

5 For more on this understanding of the Levitical system, see L. Michael Morales, *Who Shall Ascend the Mountain of the Lord?* (Leicester, UK: Apollos, 2015).

6 For a more detailed examination of this and other passages, see *Reformation Worship: Liturgies from the Past for the Present*, ed. Jonathan Gibson and Mark Earngey (Greensboro, NC: New Growth Press, 2018).

7 Herman Bavinck, *Reformed Dogmatics*, ed. John Bolt, trans. John Vriend (Grand Rapids: Baker Academic, 2008), 4:447.

8 For more on this understanding of preaching, and particularly the ongoing prophetic work of Christ, see Jonty Rhodes, *Man of Sorrows, King of Glory: What the Humiliation and Exaltation of Jesus Mean for Us* (Wheaton: Crossway, 2021), 121–24.

9 "The Second Helvetic Confession," chap. 1 in *Reformed Confessions of the 16th and 17th Century in English Translation*, vol. 2,

　　　1552–1566, ed. James Dennison Jr. (Grand Rapids: Reformation Heritage Books, 2010), 811.

10　Jonathan Landry Cruse, *What Happens When We Worship* (Grand Rapids: Reformation Heritage Books, 2020), 107–22.

11　John Calvin, *Institutes of the Christian Religion,* ed. John T. McNeill, trans. Ford Lewis Battles (London: Westminster John Knox Press), 4.14.17.

Questions and Answers on Reformed Worship

　1　I'm grateful to my friend Matt Searles for these insights on psalm singing.

Also from P&R Publishing

The Gospel of Jesus weaves the entirety of the four gospels into a continuous, highly readable harmony that can be used as a helpful Bible study aid. With marginal references and clearly indicated editorial changes, this new giftable edition of a classic work features the modern Christian Standard Bible® translation and includes maps, dates, and locations.

"Loraine Boettner's integration of the fourfold canonical Good News helps new generations of Christians to encounter the testimony of 'the original eyewitnesses and servants of the word,' deepening our certainty in what we have been instructed (Luke 1:2). The use of the Christian Standard Bible, which happily combines accuracy with readability, makes this new edition of Boettner's harmony both edifying and pleasurable to read."
—**Dennis E. Johnson**, Professor Emeritus of Practical Theology, Westminster Seminary California

If you find this book helpful, consider writing a review online —or contact P&R at editorial@prpbooks.com with your comments. We'd love to hear from you.